SIMPLY PRAYER

JOINING GOD
FOR THE
REST OF YOUR LIFE

BILL ELLIFF

SIMPLY PRAYER: Joining God for the Rest of Your Life
By Bill Elliff

Published by TruthINK Publications
6600 Crystal Hill Road
North Little Rock, Arkansas 72118

Cover Design | Keith Runkle

ISBN: 978-0-9831168-6-8

Printed in the United States of America

Scripture quotations taken from the New American Standard Bible Updated, Copyright © 1960, 1962, 1963, 1968, 1971, 1972, 1973, 1975, 1977, 1995 by The Lockman Foundation. Used by permission. (www.Lockman.org), *unless otherwise noted.*

WHY READ THIS BOOK?

Simply Prayer by my friend, Bill Elliff is a book I will return to again and again. It is filled with great teaching, great stories, but most of all great heart! You will be led by the Spirit to stop and pray numerous times as you read this book. Thank you Bill, for sharing your heart for intimacy with the Lord in prayer with us.

Dave Butts
Chairman, America's National Prayer Committee

We need to be inspired to pray. *Simply Prayer* will inspire you to pray more consistently, more powerfully, and more effectively. Thank you Bill Elliff for inspiring us to pray by recounting the stories of God's mighty works in the Bible, in ancient history, in modern history, and in today's living history as we are living through these unprecedented times. This is why we need to share *Simply Prayer* with Christ-followers everywhere.

Dr. Ronnie Floyd
President & CEO, Southern Baptist Convention Executive Committee

My Grandmother loved to cook. I cherished the aroma of her home. When I crossed the threshold of her house I was transported: at home where I belonged; my priorities clarified, and surrounded by the provisions and affections of those who defined me and loved me.

Simply Prayer accomplishes the same. Entering in, we're met with the aroma of God. We know at once where we belong—at home in the house of prayer where God, the fellowship of God's Spirit, the promises of God, the power of God, the feast of his mercies, the union of his family, and his purposes on earth and in heaven all meet around the same table. I commend it.

Bob Bakke
Senior Pastor, Hillside Church, Bloomington, MN

So thankful for Bill Elliff's new book. At Hope Church we have learned that when we seek God in prayer, we experience God in power. *Simply Prayer* is a practical guide to help us all discover greater ways to seek God in prayer both powerfully and effectively. Having known Bill personally for years, I am thankful that this is not a book of theory. It is a book born out of Bill's lifelong journey of cultivating the practice of "praying without ceasing." I highly recommend this book to anyone desperate to experience God's activity in and through their life!

Vance Pittman
Senior Pastor, Hope Church, Las Vegas, NV

Do you struggle developing a consistent, meaningful, intimate prayer life? My friend and mentor, Bill Elliff, has put together some easy-to-understand biblical insights from his own spiritual journey that can transform your relationship with Jesus. If practiced from a humble and obedient heart, it will lead to an experience with God our Father that you previously thought impossible. I encourage you to take time to read and digest this short book. Then, get ready to experience some powerful encounters with the One who knows, hears, and answers our deepest longings.

Byron Paulus
Executive Director/CEO, Life Action Ministries. Founder, OneCry

Bill Elliff's practical pastoral wisdom has enriched my life in countless ways and over many years. *Simply Prayer* is another treasure of truth birthed out of Bill's life-long passion to seek God. If you want practical and proven guidance to ignite a fresh experience of prayer this book will take you there.

Daniel Henderson
President, Strategic Renewal International
Author of Transforming Prayer: How Everything Changes When You Seek God's Face

The beauty of *Simply Prayer* is that it is **simple,** and it describes the essence of **prayer**. Bill Elliff strips away the superficial and shows us the fundamental nature, power, character and beauty of prayer. It's a must read for every believer wanting to become a man or woman of prayer. If you want to know why and how we should pray, then read *Simply Prayer*. You'll be amazed to learn how simple and powerful prayer really is.

Sammy Tippit,

International Evangelist and Author of The Coronavirus Pandemic and Prayer

Such a needed, clear and fresh approach to the much-neglected discipline of prayer. The author's assertion that "prayer was never meant to be merely a side room, but the foundation of the church," is a graphic verbal depiction of what our praying will become if we will embrace the simple praying habits urged upon us in these pages.

Tom Elliff

Pastor and former President of the International Mission Board, SBC

When Bill Elliff talks about prayer I listen and I learn. *Simply Prayer* is practical—excellent for anyone wanting to pray more and better. *Simply Prayer* is also provocative—as I read it I found myself repeatedly stopping to pray! I encourage you to read it and put it in practice.

J. Kie Bowman

Senior Pastor, Hyde Park Baptist Church, Austin, Texas

Unceasing Prayer Movement

Few things are more needed today than people of prayer. And few people are better at encouraging and equipping us to be people of prayer than my good friend, Bill Elliff. His prayer insight has helped many—and can help you—find what every heart longs for: a more fulfilling connection to our Lord!

Dr. Robert Lewis

Pastor, Founder—Men's Fraternity/BetterMan

Simply Prayer is a delightful read. It is engaging. Practical. Useful without being merely pragmatic. It is profoundly simple without lacking depth. It is challenging, even convicting, and yet it is written in a spirit of grace. It's "Pastor" Bill Elliff, maybe at his best!

Dr. P. Douglas Small, CCU
President-Project Pray; Prayer Coordinator for the Church of God

The underground stream that runs through Bill Elliff's life flows as well through this stimulating book on prayer. Do you need motivation to pray? What about guidance on what to pray? Here are encouraging words to help you become the pray-er you have always wanted to be.

Jim Elliff
Christian Communicators Worldwide

Some things God will do whether you pray or not. But some things God will only do when you pray. Of all the spiritual disciplines, prayer is the most powerful. My friend, Bill Elliff, is a prayer-warrior. His new book, *Simply Prayer*, tells you why and how to pray. If you're ready to go to the next level in your prayer life, this book will lead you upward to the throne of God.

Steve Gaines, PhD
Pastor, Bellevue Baptist Church, Memphis, TN

Some write about something they've learned, others about something they've lived. As someone that knows the writer, be assured that Bill has given us both. He's spent a lifetime learning how to pray and then strived to live out what he's learned. I know of no one that's a better authority on the subject! This book will help make the mystical, simple while building our faith for the supernatural. A better prayer life is waiting for you. Go on the journey because your prayers matter.

Kyle Reno
Directional Pastor, The Summit Church, Little Rock, AR

Simply Prayer is a must read if you seriously want to understand foundational truths for an effective, ongoing prayer life. A few years ago, Bill taught much of this material in a weekend prayer conference at Sherwood. These truths reignited our prayer ministry and led to a new vision statement at Sherwood, establishing our ministry from a prayer base, not a prayer afterthought. I will be forever indebted to Bill for helping us frame our thinking and embrace extraordinary praying. Bill doesn't just write about prayer, he is a man of prayer.

Michael Catt, Senior Pastor, Sherwood Baptist Church, Albany, Georgia Executive Producer, Sherwood Films

Besides faithfulness to Scripture, the best test of a book on prayer is whether it makes you want to pray. This book succeeds on both counts. Pastors and laypeople, adults and teenagers, mature believers and new followers of Jesus can all profit from reading *Simply Prayer*. It is clear, practical, and encouraging. I'm so glad I read this book!

Donald S. Whitney, Professor of Biblical Spirituality and Assoc. Dean at The Southern Baptist Theological Seminary. Author of "Spiritual Disciplines for the Christian Life" and "Praying the Bible."

I have known Bill Elliff for 50 years. This book represents the passion of his heart. He lives these words every day. *Simply Prayer* is practical, powerful and personal. If you want to become fully present to the presence of God in your life, *Simply Prayer* is a must read.

Bill Wellons, A Founding Pastor of Fellowship Bible Church, Little Rock, AR. Director of the Leadership Residency Program for Church Planters, Fellowship Associates

I could not put it down! Do NOT underestimate the title. *Simply Prayer: Joining God for the Rest of Your Life* is truly simple, but a potent and powerful word for the whole church in a strategic moment of church history.

Dr. Ralph W. Neighbour III

Team Leader, Revitalization, California Southern Baptist Convention.

TABLE OF CONTENTS

Dedicated to my mother, Jewell Carter Elliff,
the most precious, powerful intercessor in our family line.
She loved Jesus and simply prayed.

BEFORE YOU BEGIN ...

MY DEAR FRIEND AND MENTOR, Ron Dunn, was visiting Scotland with his wife, Kay. They had rented a car but had to pay careful attention. In Scotland, they drive on the left side of the road, not the right as he was accustomed.

They were doing fine until they came to a stoplight and began talking. Soon the light changed and, turning the corner, Ron instinctively went to the right-hand side of the road. He looked up and saw a car coming at him in his lane.

"Look at that idiot!" he said to his wife.

"Wrong idiot," Kay replied. "Move over!"

Ron would later say that he didn't intend to go to the wrong side, but it was simply natural because he had driven there so many years.

We have driven on the wrong side for a long time. Because of this, prayer is an unnatural lane to us. This is why we must *learn* how to pray. Years of sporadic communication with God and independent decisions have formed deep ruts in our souls. Our normal tendency is to lean on our own understanding and not even acknowledge God. Most people live days, weeks, even years without ever consulting the One who made them. They live prayerless lives, only coming to God when they are in a crisis. In moments of deep need, they find it hard to communicate with Him because of their lack of regular prayer. God is there, but they don't know how to enter His presence and talk to Him.

I went to college during the Jesus Movement in the early 1970s. There was an atmospheric sense of God's presence and my friends and I found ourselves often in prayer, sometimes all night. We watched God move in answer to our fumbling but zealous college requests. We were awed to discover God doing in a matter of moments things that our best efforts couldn't accomplish in years.

The summer after my freshman year, my brother, Jim, and I went to Seattle, Washington, for eight weeks to lead youth revivals in churches. We began to pray together daily prior to our leaving for Seattle. One day Jim said, "Let's just pray nothing but Scripture." We began and continued throughout the summer and discovered dimensions of Scripture-based praying that we had never known. This was another profound lesson in prayer that would affect me for the rest of my life.

I was learning the value and joy of daily Bible study, but I longed to pray more. As I studied the lives of great Christian men and women, I noticed the prevailing theme of a prayer-filled life. Convicted by 1 Thessalonians 5:17, I began to pray a simple prayer, which I have continued to pray for over 50 years:

"Father, please make me a man of unceasing prayer."

I have read countless books on prayer, which all benefited me. But the greatest classroom for prayer is praying. By His grace, He has allowed me (and you) the highest privilege: we can enter into His presence and commune with Him! To fail in prayer is to miss the greatest joy and lose our greatest power.

This book is borne out of a 50-year quest to experience God's presence in prayer. My great desire is that you would read it and let it stimulate you to greater prayer. May it lead you into the Throne Room to enjoy a lifetime of communion with the One who knows and loves you best. He's been waiting for you to come.

Bill Elliff

Little Rock, Arkansas

May 7, 2020

*Please notice that there are questions for group discussion or private reflection included at the end of the book.

CHAPTER 1

WHY PRAY?

AN AIRPLANE RIDE TAUGHT ME a profound truth. I was seated early on the plane, watching people as they entered. I casually looked diagonally in front of me and there was a businessman who looked to be of some importance. As I observed his expensive suit, costly watch, and high-powered business magazine I thought, "This man probably leads a lot of people. I bet he is a powerful man."

Suddenly I thought, "I wonder who is the most powerful person on this plane?" Within five seconds I knew the answer. I think it was God's Spirit who whispered this thought to my heart ...

The most powerful person in the room is the one who prays.

It made perfect sense. Everybody on the plane had natural talents and abilities. Some I'm sure had great opportunities to influence others. But the most powerful person on the plane was the man or woman who had learned how to lay hold of heaven. The person who, at any moment, could bring God into the equation with all the resources of eternity.

I looked behind me and there was a young man covered with tattoos. "It might be him," the Spirit whispered to my heart. He may be a man who, early on, has come to see the weakness of his flesh and the need for unceasing prayer.

Seated in front of me was a silver-haired grandmother. But it's probably her, I thought. Age has a way of defining our priorities.

The greatest men and women among us are those who pray. They are not like others who think they can make it on their own. Those who pray consistently understand their limitations and know how desperately they need God. Year-by-year they have cried out to God and learned to pray by praying. And each year, prayer has become increasingly important and foundational.

YOUR VALUES DETERMINE YOUR PRAYING

Everything you do is based on value. If you think exercise or reading or entertainment will bring meaning to your life, you will spend huge amounts of time there. If you think those things are worthless, you'll give your attention to something else.

The Bible speaks of prayer over 650 times with 450 recorded answers to prayer. It is one of the most oft-repeated commands in the Scripture, both by directives and examples. It is not peripheral, but foundational in our walk with Christ. And yet, most people would be honest to admit that their prayer life is weak at best. Most say they pray, but their prayers are often only in times of crisis or a fleeting prayer during the day. They nod with their heads at its value but are seldom on their knees.

Why do we have such a struggle with prayer? We don't really believe it's valuable. There could be several reasons for this tragic misunderstanding.

- LACK OF TRAINING: Perhaps no one has ever taught us how to pray meaningfully.

- BOREDOM: We have been in prayer gatherings that have been poorly led and lifeless. Prayer seems meaningless.

- FAILURE: We have tried to pray and failed. Our attention span is short. We've given up on prayer because we don't think we can do it well.

- COMPARISON: We've heard others pray with ease and power and think such prayer is unattainable for us. We've concluded that some are special intercessors and we simply don't have that gifting.

- BUSYNESS: We have let a hectic lifestyle (which is a choice) crowd out communion with God and have failed to understand how to have a running dialogue with God about everything in our lives.

- DISAPPOINTMENT: We've prayed for something—perhaps even believing with great anticipation—and it didn't seem to work. We think God doesn't answer our prayers.

- HURT: Something has happened in our life—a tragedy, a loss, a failure—and we have come to believe that God is not good. We think He doesn't really care, so why approach One who we believe to be an unloving God in prayer? We are unwilling to trust Him, and trust is the foundation of prayer.

- UNBELIEF: We have concluded that God cannot do what He has promised.

Do any of these resonate with you? If so, this book is for you. Our great need is to be overwhelmed with the inestimable value of prayer. If we understand its true worth and could find a path to pray effectively and powerfully, we will have no problem fulfilling this life-changing command from God ...

Pray without ceasing.[1]

You may be thinking "Without ceasing? I hardly pray at all. How could I possibly pray continually throughout each day?"

It's not only possible, but it's also exactly what God desires. He has great plans for us and for His kingdom that can only be accomplished if we will continually communicate with Him.

So, why should we value prayer? Why should we seek to become men or women of unceasing prayer?

GOD WANTS YOUR PRAYERS

"Pray without ceasing" is not a nice thought from God, it's a command. God is telling us to pray and to pray with no intermission. It is hard to believe, but God wants to communicate with you more than you want to communicate with Him. How could this possibly be true?

God Loves You and Wants to Talk with You!

"What comes into our minds when we think about God is the most important thing about us," said A.W. Tozer.[2] Nowhere is

---

[1] 1 Thessalonians 5:17
[2] A.W. Tozer, *Knowledge of the Holy*

this more true than in prayer. Our view of prayer is dramatically affected by our view of God's character—particularly of His love. If we have a low view of God's love for us, we will see our prayers as unimportant to Him. But if we understand the magnitude of His affection for His children, we will realize how much God longs for us to come to Him.

I have eight married children who have produced 20 grandchildren (and counting!). I'm far from a perfect Grandad. But my heart leaps every time the door opens and one of my kids or grandkids comes charging into the room. I love them! I want to know about their lives and be involved in their decisions. I want them to call me when they are in need. I'm concerned when I haven't heard from them. I'm honored as they ask for my advice. I'm thrilled when I hear of their successes and saddened by their difficulties.

What touches them, touches me. If this is true of me in my imperfection, it is perfectly true of our Father in the perfection of His compassion. "The Lord will accomplish that which concerns me. Your lovingkindness is everlasting," said the Psalmist.[3] What touches us, touches the Father as He longs to be involved in every detail of our lives.

God Made You and Knows Your Life Won't Work Without Him.

God has designed your body with incredible precision. Every part, down to the smallest cell, is interconnected and dependent upon the other parts. You cannot survive without your heart, or your

---

[3] Psalm 135:8

lungs, or your kidneys. And each of these organs communicates with the others. This interconnectedness is essential.

God made us physically but also designed us spiritually, and He never intended for us to live without Him.

> God made us: invented us as a man invents an engine. A car is made to run on petrol, and it would not run properly on anything else. Now God designed the human machine to run on Himself. He Himself is the fuel our spirits were designed to burn, or the food our spirits were designed to feed on. There is no other.[4]

Like the relationship of branches to a life-giving vine, we must remain in continual union with Him, just as Christ said. Prayer is the means of this abiding connection.

> *Abide in Me, and I in you. As the branch cannot bear fruit of itself unless it abides in the vine, so neither can you unless you abide in Me. I am the vine, you are the branches; he who abides in Me and I in him, he bears much fruit, for apart from Me you can do nothing. If anyone does not abide in Me, he is thrown away as a branch and dries up; and they gather them, and cast them into the fire and they are burned. If you abide in Me, and My words abide in you, ask whatever you wish, and it will be done for you.[5]*

Your answer to one question will instantly reveal whether you are abiding in humble union with Christ or if you are so proud that

---

[4] C.S. Lewis, *Mere Christianity*
[5] John 15:4-7

you feel you do not need Him. Remember, God resists the proud man but pours out His grace on the humble.[6] Here is the revealing question:

How much do you pray?

Not merely perfunctory prayers ("Lord, bless this food to the nourishment of my body"), but how often do you rise in the morning, slip to your knees by your bed and cry out, "Lord, I cannot survive today without You!" For if you can go a day or a week without prayer, it illustrates that you believe you can make it without Him.

God knows you need Him, even if you don't recognize this reality. That's why He's gone to such incredible lengths to make it possible for you to talk with Him all day, every day for the rest of your life and beyond!

God Is Training You and Prayer Interprets All of Life.

From the beginning of life until the end, each joy and crisis, hard moment and happy experience, can yield seasons of spiritual development. God wastes nothing with His children. Like a good parent, He uses every moment of the common day to raise us to the "measure of the stature of the fullness of Christ."[7]

My brother-in-law once bought an old 1931 Chevrolet. It was in terrible condition, but he desired to restore it to its former beauty. It sat like an eyesore in their yard for years (to my sister Sandy's great annoyance). Finally, he had the means to bring it back to life. When he did, it was stunning! It looked and ran just

---

[6]James 4:6
[7]Ephesians 4:12

as it did when it came off the assembly line. Everything, even down to the paint color, was just as it was created.

All of us have been wrecked and damaged by sin. We don't work right. We've "fallen short of the glory of God."[8] We are crippled by our disconnection from God and His original plans for us. God intends to restore us to the Manufacturer's original specifications and He often uses mighty blows to reshape us. At times it is excruciatingly painful.

If we are not listening to God through His Word and prayer, we misinterpret the purpose of His work. We unknowingly adopt the world's evaluations of these events. We can get angry at difficulties, even blaming God. We become confused about our lives, not understanding each circumstance's purposes.

But when we are listening to Him through His Word and prayer, we begin to understand what He is doing: that all things can work together for our good to conform us to the image of His Son.[9] That God is God and He has a right to do what He desires, but that He is also good and He always does what is best. That every blow of His transforming work is motivated by transcendent love.

Those of us who are praying hear His voice intimately and understand His designs. And, our souls find our rest in Him. We realize life is more than our earthly days and that He is preparing us to rule and reign with Him in eternity. As we more fully realize this, we are awed by His purposes and overwhelmed by His care.

Do you understand how deeply God loves you and that He is waiting to talk with you all day long, every day? That the God of the Universe longs to be with you, interpreting all of life's experiences?

---

[8]Romans 3:23
[9]Romans 8:28-29

But there are other reasons why prayer is so valuable.

YOU AND OTHERS NEED YOUR PRAYERS

God has never wasted a single word. When He said, "Pray without ceasing" He knew that there were things to be accomplished in our lives and the lives of others that simply would not be accomplished any other way.

> God has of his own motion placed Himself under the law of prayer and has obligated Himself to answer the prayers of men. He has ordained prayer as a means whereby he will do things through men as they pray, which he would not otherwise do. If prayer puts God to work on earth, then, by the same token, prayerlessness rules God out of the world's affairs and prevents him from working.[10]

Can you imagine discovering in heaven one day that God wanted to accomplish much more through you, but didn't because you didn't pray? There were missed opportunities, lives that could have been changed, freedom from sin, a perfect provision that was not realized.

We must understand what prayer does for us and others that cannot be obtained by any other means.

Prayer Brings God into the Equation

My oldest son-in-law, Randy, put himself through college as a mechanic. He is now in the finance business, but I'm so grateful

---

[10] E.M. Bounds, *The Weapon of Prayer*

that he's so knowledgeable about cars. With eight kids, I bought multiple "college cars" that were eternally breaking down. Here's how the phone calls usually went from my children:

"Dad, I'm stuck on the side of the road."

"Did you check the oil?" I ask (the only thing I really know to do).

"Yes, it seems fine."

"Have you called Randy?"

"No, not yet; I wanted to call you first."

"Why are you calling me when I know nothing about cars? Call Randy. Quick!"

When I am brought into the car equation, it yields little help. But when Randy gets on the phone it "availeth much!" The presence of Randy's advice changes everything

Do you want to handle everything by yourself? Is the situation best resolved by your limited understanding and resources? Prayerlessness indicates this unwise decision. Cut through the middleman (yourself and your merely human thinking) and go right to God in prayer.

Do you want others you love stranded without God's help? If not, begin to pray, for prayer brings God into the equation of their lives. Without prayer, they get what they can do. With prayer, they get what God can do. It just makes sense to pray without ceasing.

One of the great missionaries from our church, Tory Lewis, once wrote:

> I am learning now more than ever that prayer IS the work. We want so much to see a multiplying move-

ment among our people, but no matter how many small groups we start, we will never see true growth, and certainly not multiplication, without the Holy Spirit's say so. And so we find ourselves on our knees, begging for God to move and to keep us out of the way.

Prayer Re-orients You to Heaven's Perspective

To hungry ants, a log in the road seems like an insurmountable obstacle to get to their food on the other side. But to us, it's a simple step. If the ants could see from our perspective, they would have faith to believe it was possible.

Those who are prayerless look at life from the bottom up. Hills are bigger, mountains are higher, obstacles are daunting. If, however, we are often in Scripture-fed prayer, we begin to see life from God's perspective. We see His agenda and His power. We realize the mountain in front of us is nothing for God.

This is why Paul reminds us to lift up our eyes. The only means of doing this is through His Word and prayer.

> *Therefore if you have been raised up with Christ, keep seeking the things above, where Christ is, seated at the right hand of God. Set your mind on the things above, not on the things that are on earth. For you have died and your life is hidden with Christ in God.*[11]

Jesus continually reminded us to open our ears and hear and our eyes and see. If you want His heavenly vision to permeate your

---

[11] Colossians 3:1-3

heart and enlarge your faith, you must pray!

PRAYER CALMS YOUR HEART AND BRINGS PEACE

Life is hard. It provides manifold opportunities for anxiety and fear. Many people live in a constant state of worry. Every day piles on more and the anxiety can build to full-fledged depression. Is there a remedy? How is it possible to find peace, even during a storm?

> *Be anxious for nothing, but in everything by prayer and supplication with thanksgiving let your requests be made known to God. And the peace of God, which surpasses all comprehension, will guard your hearts and your minds in Christ Jesus.*[12]

Prayer changes us. Prayer allows us to hear the Master's voice and see His perfect plans. And God promises (both here and in many other passages) that prayer releases our burdens and brings incomprehensible peace. Steve Brown said, "Not being changed by prayer is sort of like standing in the middle of a spring rain without getting wet. It's hard to stand in the center of God's acceptance and love without getting it all over you."[13]

If you want to live the remainder of your life with unceasing worry, don't pray. But if you long for unceasing peace, you must learn how to live in unceasing prayer.

---

[12] Philippians 4:6-7
[13] Steve Brown

Prayer Aligns You to God's Perfect Will

The greatest battle of Jesus' life was fought in the Garden of Geth-semane several hours before the Cross. Jesus knew what He was about to face. The physical suffering would be excruciating, but far worse would be this: "God made Him who knew no sin to be sin on our behalf."[14] The perfectly Pure-One would bear the full weight of the judgment of the Father. The One who had been in eternal union with His Father would endure the penalty of being separated from Him. "My God, my God, why have you forsaken Me?"[15] would be His agonizing cry.

The battle for our souls was won in prayer. In agony, Jesus asked God to use any other means, if possible, to accomplish His plan for our salvation. But in prayer, the will of Christ was completely submitted to the will of His Father. "Not my will, but Thine be done," was His cry.[16]

This is our greatest problem, isn't it? We want what we want and it's usually not the best for us. How is this changed? Standing before our Heavenly Father in prayer we understand the perfection of His love and plans. We realize His will is good, acceptable, and perfect and our will becomes aligned with His. Our prayer becomes "THY kingdom come, THY will be done."[17]

Prayer is not about getting God to do what we want. It is getting us to a place where we want what He wants, which is always best. My brother, Tom, once said, "If a man can ever come to the point where all he wants is all God wants, then all

---

[14] 2 Corinthians 5:21
[15] Matthew 27:46
[16] Luke 22:42
[17] Matthew 6:10

his life he'll have all he wants, and God will have all He wants of him."

And there is one final reason we must pray without ceasing ...

SATAN FEARS YOUR PRAYERS

We have a terribly powerful Enemy. Paul reminds us of the might of our adversary in his instructions to the church at Ephesus.

> *Put on the full armor of God, so that you will be able to stand firm against the schemes of the devil. For our struggle is not against flesh and blood, but against the rulers, against the powers, against the world forces of this darkness, against the spiritual forces of wickedness in the heavenly places.*[18]

Although our enemies are powerful, we are in a winnable battle. But we must prepare ourselves with the armor God provides. Once armed, there is something proactive we must do.

> *With all prayer and petition pray at all times in the Spirit, and with this in view, be on the alert with all perseverance and petition for all the saints.*[19]

Unceasing prayer is the offensive weapon that wins the day. Prayer makes us see the real battle, aligns us with God's battle plan, and releases the resources of heaven. The Enemy is powerless against a man or woman of unceasing prayer.

---

[18] Ephesians 6:11-12
[19] Ephesians 6:18

"Satan dreads nothing but prayer. His one concern
is to keep the saints from praying. He fears nothing
from prayerless studies, prayerless work, prayerless
religion. He laughs at our toil, he mocks our wisdom,
but he trembles when we pray."[20]

John Piper reminds us that prayer is our means of communication
in this battle. If the communication lines are cut, we are powerless
before the Enemy.

The number one reason why prayer malfunctions
in the hands of believers is that they try to turn a
wartime walkie-talkie into a domestic intercom. Until
you believe that life is war, you cannot know what
prayer is for. Prayer is for the accomplishment of a
wartime mission.

It is as though the field commander (Jesus) called in
the troops, gave them a crucial mission ("Go and bear
fruit"), handed each of them a personal transmitter
coded to the frequency of the General's headquarters,
and said, "Comrades, the General has a mission for
you. He aims to see it accomplished. And to that end,
he has authorized me to give each of you personal
access to him through these transmitters. If you stay
true to his mission and seek his victory first, he will
always be as close as your transmitter, to give tactical
advice and to send in air cover when you or your
comrades need it."

[20] Samuel Chadwick, *The Path of Prayer*

But what have millions of Christians done? They have stopped believing that we are in a war. No urgency, no watching, no vigilance, no strategic planning. Just easy peacetime and prosperity. And what did they do with the walkie-talkie? They tried to rig it up as an intercom in their cushy houses and cabins and boats and cars—not to call in firepower for conflict with a mortal enemy, but to ask the maid to bring another pillow to the den.[21]

Why should you give your life to the pursuit of unceasing prayer? God wants your prayers, you and others need your prayers, and Satan fears your prayers. And there's one more consideration: PRAYER WORKS! Millions of illustrations can be given from Scripture and human experience.

If we want to know God and engage in what matters, we will give ourselves to this life-changing task. God will help us get there, but we must begin the journey to become men and women of unceasing prayer.

What the church needs today is not more machinery or better, not new organizations or more and novel methods, but men whom the Holy Ghost can use—men of prayer, men mighty in prayer. The Holy Ghost does not flow through methods, but through men. He does not come on machinery, but on men. He does not anoint plans, but men—men of prayer.[22]

---

[21]John Piper, *Prayer, the Work of Missions*
[22]E.M. Bounds, *Power Through Prayer*

CHAPTER 2

HOW DO WE ENTER IN?

"MY PRAYERS SEEM LIKE they hit the ceiling and bounce right back at me," said one discouraged man. We all understand this. There's nothing more disheartening than disconnected prayer. It's the reason many have given up on intercession. Full of fresh resolve, they jump into prayer but never find a real sense of God's presence. It seems like they are talking into the air. A steady diet of such prayer will make them spiritually confused and before long, they'll stop praying altogether.

Such praying is explainable. We have not learned how to *enter in.*

> Much of so-called prayer, both public and private, is not unto God. In order that prayer be really unto God, there must be a definite and conscious approach to God when we pray. In much of our prayer, there is little thought of God. Our mind is taken up with the thought of what we need and is not occupied with the thought of the mighty and loving Father from whom we are seeking these gifts.

If then, we would pray aright, the first thing that we should do is to see ... that we really get into His very presence. Before a word of petition is offered, we should have the definite and vivid consciousness that we are talking to God and should believe that He is listening to our petition and is going to grant the thing that we ask of Him. This is only possible by the Holy Spirit's power, so we should look to the Holy Spirit to really lead us into the presence of God and should not be hasty in words until he has actually brought us there.[23]

When Jesus gave His most comprehensive training on prayer in Matthew 6:5-15, He spent more time instructing us about how to enter into prayer than He did giving us the model prayer. But we rarely focus on these essential, preparatory elements. We charge into prayer and quickly reel off a laundry list of things we want God to do. Failing to realize Who we're approaching, we never really engage God's presence consciously. Studying Matthew 6:5-9 gives us indispensable insight about how to enter. We must learn how to approach God rightly in prayer before we pray.

WE MUST ENTER IN WITH ... SINCERITY

> *"When you pray, you are not to be like the hypocrites; for they love to stand and pray in the synagogues and on the street corners so that they may be seen by men. Truly I say to you, they have their reward in full."* [24]

---

[23] R.A. Torrey, *How to Pray*
[24] Matthew 6:5

The common practice of the religious leaders in Jesus' day was to stand in the most conspicuous places possible and pray loud prayers. Their primary intent was to be seen by men. There could be only one motivation behind this practice: PRIDE.

God is clear about what pride does in our relationship with Him. God resists the proud. He actively stands in opposition to those who approach Him in arrogance. This is even true of His children. (You will notice He's addressing believers when He says in James 4:6 that He "resists the proud but gives grace to the humble.")

Have you ever had the frustrating experience of talking to someone and quickly realizing they are looking over your shoulder? They are talking loudly, hoping to be noticed by others. You sense they are searching for the next person they can talk to—the one who they feel is more important than you.

Your instant evaluation is that this disengaged, arrogant person is a fake. They are not really interested in having a conversation with you at all. They are simply using you. Very quickly you determine that you are not going to pay attention to what they are saying.

Can you imagine doing this in the presence of the God of the Universe? And yet, this is what much of our prayers are like. Unaware of the One we are approaching, we engage in surface prayers for the sole purpose of impressing others. God does not hear nor respond to such insincerity.

We must enter into His presence with the sole desire of communing with God alone.

AS YOU ENTER...

The greatest One is before you and He's the only
audience you need.

WE MUST ENTER IN ... SECLUSION

*"But you, when you pray, go into your inner room, close
your door and pray to your Father who is in secret, and
your Father who sees what is done in secret will reward
you.*[25]

The most significant transformation in my prayer life came while
reading Dr. Martyn Lloyd-Jones' commentary on this verse.[26] Lloyd-
Jones said that when he began to understand the meaning of this
verse, he realized he could enter into his "closet" with the Lord
whether he was in his private study or standing in a crowd of
thousands. His wife would say after his death, that what she
missed most about "The Doctor's" ministry was not his preaching,
but his praying. He knew how to enter in.

God is not necessarily talking about a physical closet in this
verse. Although such a practice is fine, it is not always available.
I have a mental picture when I begin to pray that has changed
everything for me.

Imagine opening a door and stepping into a foyer ... the entrance to God's Throne Room. Now, turn behind you as you enter

---

[25] Matthew 6:6
[26] Martyn Lloyd-Jones, *The Sermon on the Mount*

and shut the door. Shut the door on others and last week and next week. Even, in a sense, shut the door on yourself. Your sole focus is the One you are about to encounter.

Next, consciously step into the Throne Room of God! You have total access here because of Jesus Christ. Paul says this well...

> *Therefore, having been justified by faith, we have peace with (literally "facing") God through our Lord Jesus Christ, through whom also we have obtained our introduction by faith into this grace in which we stand; and we exult in hope of the glory of God.*[27]

For those who have come by faith, Christ—through His death and resurrection—has taken us by the hand and walked us into the Throne Room. God is on one side, we are on the other, and Jesus has introduced us to the Father. We once were at war with the One on the throne, but now we have "peace facing God!" What a glorious privilege! What an unspeakable honor!

Pause as you enter and look around. As you gaze throughout the Throne Room, you will see Christ seated at the right hand of the Father, and you will notice that He "always lives to make intercession" for His children.[28] Angels hover around the throne. Praise is unending. Let the wonder of this environment overwhelm you. Your heart will begin to be filled with worship.

As you have entered, begin to pray. Filled with this vision, you will probably not rattle off meaningless rituals. You are going to close the door and "pray TO YOUR FATHER." There is a singular

---

[27] Romans 5:1-2 *(parenthesis added)*
[28] Hebrews 7:25

direction. You are not praying to others. Your whole vision is filled with the Almighty. You are directing your prayers to the One who is seated upon the Throne!

Rosalind Rinker said, "I have discovered that prayer's real purpose is to put God at the center of our attention and forget ourselves and the impression we are making."[29] This posture changes everything for us in prayer. We are looking at Him, and Him alone. Everything else pales in comparison to this vision.

If we will enter in like this, giving God our undivided attention, the greatest reward will be God Himself!

AS YOU ENTER...

God is waiting for you on His throne and He longs to reward you in His presence!

WE MUST ENTER IN WITH ... SIMPLICITY

> "And when you are praying, do not use meaningless repetition as the Gentiles do, for they suppose that they will be heard for their many words."[30]

Rosalind Rinker served as a missionary to China for many years. She wrote an extremely helpful book on prayer that *Christianity Today* said was one of the most influential books written in the

---

[29] Rosalind Rinker, *Prayer, Conversing with God*
[30] Matthew 6:7

last half of the 20th Century. It was entitled *Prayer, Conversing with God*. She defines prayer like this: "Prayer is the expression of the human heart in conversation with God. The more natural the prayer, the more real He becomes. Simply put: prayer is a conversation between two persons who love each other."[31]

All of us have experienced both good conversations and bad. What is true about a good conversation?

1. We become aware of and engaged with each other.

2. We take turns, both talking and listening.

3. We stay on a subject, giving our full attention to the topic at hand.

4. We speak in a common language (if we want to be understood!).

5. We are mutually concerned about each other.

What is true of a conversation with another human has applications for our conversations with God. Since we were made in His image, this would make perfect sense. A liberating experience in both personal and collective prayer is realizing we can come to Him in simplicity. For instance,

- We don't have to use special language ("Thee's" and "Thou's"). God loves hearing our normal voice and language.

- We speak to Him at our level of maturity and understanding. He loves the prayers of a new believer as well as an old saint; a 10-year-old boy or an 80-year-old grandmother.

---

[31] Rosalind Rinker, *Prayer, Conversing with God*

- We don't have to say everything we want to say to God in one long paragraph. There should be times of listening to God, pausing in His presence and hearing what He might want to say to us, reading and meditating on His Word, praying His Word back to Him, and speaking to Him about what's on our heart. And, if we're praying with others, we should pray short sections of prayer (just as we do in normal conversations) and let others join in.

- We should naturally move from one topic to the next as God directs. (We'll see that more clearly in the next chapter.)

- We should realize that God is intimately acquainted with all our ways and that He loves us greatly. He is concerned about us. This makes our prayer not merely a series of "requests" to some uncaring King, but a conversation with someone who is motivated by perfect love.

AS YOU ENTER...

God hears you and you don't have to impress Him.

WE MUST ENTER IN WITH ... SIMPLE FAITH

"So do not be like them; for your Father knows what you need before you ask Him."[32]

---

[32] Matthew 6:8

Needs should drive us to prayer. One of my mentors, Manley Beasley, used to say that "Needs are God's messenger boys, telling us that God has a supply." Our needs are caused or allowed by God to push us to Himself in faith.

Faith is God's operating system. Everything in God's relationship with man functions this way. Faith is dependency. Man has gone independent since the garden. God's great design is to bring us back to dependence upon Himself.

Evidence of this is the vast number of promises from God in the Bible (over 7,000 which is the equivalent of seven promises per page!). God says, "I will do this if you depend upon Me." He is forcing us to faith because He has designed for us to live this way. Therefore, the promises of God are important templates for us in prayer. We can come in faith relying on these promises.

The writer of Hebrews reminds us of faith's absolute importance.

> And without faith it is impossible to please Him, for he who comes to God must believe that He is (dependency) and that He is a rewarder of those who seek Him (expectancy).[33]

When we begin to see that God uses needs to bring us to faith, we see all the experiences of our life differently. We can now come to Him in faith in prayer, knowing that ...

- He KNOWS our needs.

- He has PURPOSE in our needs.

---

[33] Hebrews 11:6 (parenthesis added)

- He has PROMISES related to our needs.

- He has PROVISION for our needs!

Whatever the need, we can come in faith! And faith is always rewarded by our faithful God!

AS YOU ENTER...

Pray in faith, for God already knows your needs and has perfect provisions prepared.

WE MUST ENTER IN AS ... SONS AND DAUGHTERS!

> *"Pray, then, in this way: 'Our Father who is in heaven, hallowed be Your name."*[34]

It is important to note that Christ's instructions to us as we begin to pray to God is not to address Him as ...

- Our JUDGE who is in heaven

- Our OMNIPOTENT LEADER who in heaven

- Our KING who is in heaven

- Our MASTER who is in heaven

---

[34]Matthew 6:9a

Any of these titles would be accurate. But Christ is very deliberate. He tells us to approach God as our FATHER. This means that, by God's grace through faith, we have been adopted into the family. We are His sons and daughters.

But this is not just any father. It is our Father who is in heaven. This is a Father with ultimate provisions. He holds the stars in His hands. He is the One who owns the cattle on a thousand hills. He knows our needs before we mention them and is perfect in His love and overflowing in His generosity. He is the One who sees time and eternity at a glance and is the Sovereign Ruler over heaven and earth.

If you are a follower of Christ, He is YOUR Father, and He invites you to address Him with this endearing term. As one of His children, you can come in prayer realizing ...

- You have the best Father!

- He cares about you as only a perfect Father can.

- He is continually committed to you (for all of eternity).

- He will never leave you or forsake you.

- Your sin grieves Him and must be dealt with, but it doesn't change His commitment to you.

- He knows how everything He has for you will train and perfect you.

- As your Father, these moments in prayer are more precious to Him than they are to you!

Our prayers are not a meaningless ritual before a harsh God. It is a tender conversation between two who love each other.

AS YOU ENTER...

Your Father loves you and is waiting for you!

I have prayed with a great African-American pastor, Kevin Kelly, in our city for almost 30 years. He is tremendous man of God who understands prayer and has been a spiritual force in our region for several decades.

Once he and I were leading a citywide prayer gathering. As the people began to pray, one of his older ladies began to pray loudly. He turned to me on the stage and said, "That's Sister (name)." I nodded my head.

In a moment, he said, "She's a Mother of the church." I understood that endearing term which meant a distinguished, godly female leader.

In a moment, she began to pray as fervently as anyone I've ever heard. I smiled as Kevin leaned over to me and said, "She's going in!" And she was.

There's nothing more powerful than God's presence. It should humble us to know that Christ gave His life so that we might have entrance into the Throne Room. What a tragedy it would be if it was never said of us, "He/she is going in!"

I would challenge you, right now, to lay this book aside. Take a few moments to enter into the Throne Room and shut the door. It should be a familiar place, an hourly place for you if you are to pray without ceasing. Enter in with sincerity, seclusion, simplicity, and simple faith as a Son or Daughter. Don't rush in His presence. It might be good to bring no requests to Him at first. Simply get acclimated to His presence. Sense the reality of the moment. Enjoy the privilege of being with Him. Worship Him and then ask Him if there is anything He wants to say to you.

Enter in with this approach, as Christ directed, each time you pray. There is simply no better place to be in heaven or earth. And, it's available to His children all the time!

CHAPTER 3

WHAT DO WE PRAY?

IT WAS MY MOST AWKWARD MOMENT. Billy Graham was coming to lead a crusade in Oklahoma City, Oklahoma, where I pastored and I was enlisted to lead a committee in preparation. One day I received an invitation to have lunch with Dr. Graham at the Governor's Mansion. I thought I would be hidden among hundreds of people, but to my surprise when I arrived, there were only 25 leaders and their spouses.

As we were mixing in the lobby for a few minutes my wife whispered, "Do you want to meet Billy Graham?"

"Absolutely!" I said.

"He's right behind you!"

I turned around and there stood a 6'2" man with broad shoulders who was the greatest evangelist in the world. I stared at him ("gawked" might be a better word) and went speechless. He looked at me for an awkward moment and finally extended his hand and said, "I'm Billy Graham." To which I replied, "I'm Billy Elliff!" Not another word would come out of my mouth! Somehow, I couldn't muster another thought and he turned and walked away. It's one of my greatest regrets that I couldn't carry on a conversation with this great man during the one opportunity I would have in this life.

BEFORE THE KING

Most people don't know what to say when they come into the Throne Room and stand before the King of kings. We may feel awkward, confused, intimidated … maybe even speechless. We may be clueless about how to start the conversation.

That's why Christ gave us clear, simple instructions in what we often call "The Lord's Prayer" or "The Model Prayer" in Matthew 6:9-13. In six broad categories, He trains us in this most important of conversations. If we understand these six areas of prayer and begin to pray in this way, we will never lack in our conversation with God again. These verses are not intended just to pray word-for-word (which is good at times) but are designed to give us the general themes or movements of prayer. Study these verses carefully so you can understand the progression. Pray through this pattern until it becomes habitual to you.

Prayer Movement 1: ADORATION

"Our Father who is in heaven, hallowed be Your name."[35]

Christ could have instructed us to use any of the multiple names of God as we approach God's Throne. But, as we have already seen, He instructs us to use the words "our Father." We are approaching the One who has adopted us by His grace into His family. Who sent His Son to rescue us. The One who loves us perfectly. The One who cares for us more than the greatest father on earth. It is an endearing, non-threatening term as we come before God. It is

---

[35] Matthew 6:9

intended to help us realize that we are standing before Him as His beloved son or daughter.

Pause right now, put the book in your lap and look up to God and speak these words slowly before the Throne: "My Father!" and simply rest in all that means.

> If you want to make contact with God, and if you want to feel His everlasting arms about you, put your hand upon your mouth for a moment as you enter in ... Stop for a moment and remind yourself of what you are about to do. Do you know that the essence of true prayer is found in the two words "Our Father?" I suggest that if you can say from your heart whatever your condition, "My Father" in a sense your prayer is already answered.[36]

But Christ did not stop there. We are to pray "Our Father, who is in heaven." This is not just any father. Your Father is the One who is above all. He is perfect in all His ways. He is all-powerful and all-knowing. He knows every star by name. He created every cell in your body. He owns everything. There is nothing that is not at His disposal. He is the source of every provision and the giver and guarantor of every promise. He is your heavenly Father with all the resources of heaven and earth at His disposal.

As we meditate on the privilege of calling God our Father, gratitude should rise in our hearts. We should begin to realize who He is, what He has done, and that He now invites us in to talk with Him. I cannot imagine instantly praying a list of requests at

---

[36] Martyn Lloyd-Jones, *The Sermon on the Mount*

such a moment. If we have genuinely entered in, our first response will be worship. "Hallowed be Your name."

I carry several names that describe me: Bill Elliff, husband, dad, grandad, pastor, writer. You can go through my names quickly. But God's names are inexhaustible. That's why the Bible (and our heart when we meditate on Him) is filled with a multitude of names. These are given to help us understand His nature, but also to verbalize our praise in prayer.

As you enter in before the Throne, pause and spend time adoring Him. Thank Him for His great names and rehearse what you are seeing in His presence. Thank Him for who He is, but also for what He has done. If you have approached the Throne rightly, you will be overwhelmed with gratitude. Don't rush this moment in prayer. It will set the tone for the rest of your praying. Let a vision of God fill your soul and direct your praise. Don't move forward in petitions until you have hallowed Him in praise!

ADORATION

What do I notice about Him in His presence today?

Prayer Movement 2: ALIGNMENT

> *"Your kingdom come, Your will be done in earth as it is in heaven."*[37]

---

[37] Matthew 6:10

Every follower of Christ lives in two worlds, whether they realize it or not. Once we were aligned only to the material world (what we could see, feel, taste, touch, and hear). Now, we can see both material and spiritual. Before Christ, we were "dead in our trespasses and sin" and walked "according to the course of this world, according to the prince of the power of the air."[38] But now, we have been transferred from the "kingdom of darkness into the kingdom of God's dear Son!"[39]

Because of this real-time, dual citizenship, we can see and hear from God through His Word and prayer unlike those without Christ. We can see what God is doing in heaven and align ourselves with His will. Paul tells us what this advantage brings and where we should fix our gaze in prayer.

> Therefore, if you have been raised up with Christ, keep seeking the things above, where Christ is, seated at the right hand of God. Set your mind on the things above, not on the things that are on earth. For you have died and your life is hidden with Christ in God. When Christ, who is our life, is revealed, then you also will be revealed with Him in glory.[40]

Do you understand what this means? You have two residences—one on earth and one in heaven—and you can move from one to the other. As we pray, we are listening to God, seeing what He desires, and then praying His kingdom and will down to earth.

---

[38] Ephesians 2:1-2
[39] Colossians 1:13
[40] Colossians 3:1-4

Jesus showed us how this works when He chose to operate as a man on earth for 33 years. He listened to the Father in prayer and then did only what the Father initiated. These words describe why His earthly life was so effective.

> **I can do nothing on My own initiative.** As I hear, I judge and My judgment is just, because I do not seek My own will, but the will of Him who sent Me.[41]

> So Jesus said, "When you lift up the Son of Man, then you will know that I am He, and **I do nothing on My own initiative,** but I speak these things as the Father taught Me.[42]

> **For I did not speak on My own initiative,** but the Father Himself who sent Me has given Me a commandment as to what to say and what to speak.[43]

> Do you not believe that I am in the Father, and the Father is in Me? The words that I say to you **I do not speak on My own initiative,** but the Father abiding in Me does His works.[44]

Christ prayed and lived by Divine initiation and so must we! Think of how this "loop" of prayer works. We are in God's presence in prayer. We ask Him what His will is—how He wants to usher in His kingdom on earth. He reveals His will to us as He desires. We align our prayer and our lives with His will and pray for His

---

[41] John 5:30 (*emphasis added*)
[42] John 8:28 (*emphasis added*)
[43] John 12:49 (*emphasis added*)
[44] John 14:10 (*emphasis added*)

kingdom to come and His will to be done on earth as it is (being done) in heaven.

Prayer is not a matter of getting God to do what we want. It is not an exercise to persuade God to align His will with ours, but exactly the opposite. We are in His presence to hear what heaven has to say about our lives and this world. And then, in prayer, we enlist the resources of heaven to accomplish His will on earth.

This type of prayer starts in heaven, passes through the discerning intercessor, and returns to the Throne. Such prayer is effective because it was initiated by God Himself. God loves to answer His own desires, and we get the joy (and training) of being involved as His instruments.

One of my mentors, Manley Beasley, lived with three terminal illnesses in the last 20 years of his life. Once he was in the hospital and extremely sick. He suddenly sensed the presence of God in the room. Standing at the door was a woman who asked, "Are you Manley Beasley?"

"Yes," he said weakly.

"Well, I'm Corrie ten Boom," she said.

She came to his bedside and began what Manley described as the greatest prayer meeting he was ever in. She would look up to heaven and talk to God, then turn and talk to Manley. "Yes, I'll tell him that," she said as she communed with her Father and then turned to speak to Manley. She was having a normal conversation in two worlds. Soon, Manley found himself talking to Corrie and then talking to God also.

What was happening? Corrie ten Boom was standing in the Throne Room and the hospital room simultaneously, which is the birthright of every Christian. She was listening to the Father and seeing what He wanted to initiate and then bringing it to earth through prayer. Her prayers were aligning heaven and earth.

ALIGNMENT

Where is God wanting to bring in His kingdom today?

Prayer Movement 3: ACCESS

"Give us this day our daily bread."[45]

It is a mark of our independence that we never invite God into the simple, daily needs of our lives. We think we can handle things, which is our most deadly deception. Often people will say, "God is not interested in the details of my life." Apparently, they have not read their Bibles or studied the words of Christ.

> *Look at the birds of the air, that they do not sow, nor reap nor gather into barns, and yet your heavenly Father feeds them. Are you not worth much more than they? And who of you by being worried can add a single hour to his life? And why are you worried about clothing? Observe how the lilies of the field grow; they do not toil nor do they spin, yet I say to you that not even Solomon in all his glory clothed himself like one of these. But if God so clothes the grass of the field, which is alive today and tomorrow*

---

[45] Matthew 6:11

is thrown into the furnace, will He not much more clothe
you? You of little faith![46]

God cares about every part of His creation and has the capabilities
to meet our every need. But we must give Him access. We must
let Him in.

Ole Hallesby in his classic book on prayer cites Revelation 3:20
as one of the most important verses on prayer in the Bible. Christ
is speaking to the church and says, "

> *Behold, I stand at the door and knock; if anyone hears*
> *My voice and opens the door, I will come in to him and will*
> *dine with him, and he with Me."*[47]

Hallesby writes ...

> It is not our prayer which draws Jesus into our hearts.
> Nor is it our prayer which moves Jesus to come in to
> us ... All He needs is access. He enters in of His own
> accord because He desires to come in. And He enters
> in wherever He is not denied admittance ... To pray
> is nothing more involved than to let Jesus into our
> needs. To pray is to give Jesus permission to employ
> His powers in the alleviation of our distress. To pray
> is to let Jesus glorify His name in the midst of our
> needs.[48]

Christ wants us to let Him in wherever there is a need. So, Christ
tells us to pray for our "daily bread." It is beautiful in prayer to

---

[46] Matthew 6:26-30
[47] Revelation 3:20
[48] Hallesby, *Prayer*

realize that He cares about our needs—both big and small—and wants us to come to Him every day with every need.

As we let Him in, He supplies. And, since He is the sole supplier, He gets more and more glory and the world around us gains a right opinion about God.

ACCESS

What needs should I give God access to today?

Prayer Movement 4: ASSESSMENT

"Forgive us our debts as we also have forgiven our debtors"[49]

The only way we can enter into God's presence and pray is through the forgiveness purchased for us at the cross. Once we have believed in Christ and been truly converted, all the work of Calvary has been applied to our lives. Our past, present, and future sins have been forgiven.

Although these sins have been forgiven eternally, there is a need for us to address our sins before God as we commit them daily. This humbles us, reminding us of our frailty and keeps us in a right posture before God, continually maturing spiritually. The process for this daily cleansing is confession and repentance.

To confess means to "say the same thing as." If a robber has stolen something and been arrested and taken to court, he can

---

[49] Matthew 6:12

lie about his crime. He can blame others or make excuses. Or, he can confess. His confession means he has come to honest transparency as he speaks the truth about his deeds, agreeing with others who are saying he is guilty.

Proverbs says that "He who conceals his sin will not prosper, but he who confesses and forsakes them will find compassion."[50] The apostle John also addresses this continual practice.

> *If we say that we have fellowship with Him and yet walk in the darkness, we lie and do not practice the truth; but if we walk in the Light as He Himself is in the Light, we have fellowship with one another, and the blood of Jesus His Son cleanses us from all sin. If we say that we have no sin, we are deceiving ourselves and the truth is not in us. If we confess our sins, He is faithful and righteous to forgive us our sins and to cleanse us from all unrighteousness.*[51]

God hates sin because He knows what it does to His creation. He knows we will not attain perfection in this life, but He convicts us when we sin. He wants His children to walk in the light and be effective for His kingdom and experience the best in life. He desires to purge these sins from us so we can be conformed more and more to the image of His Son.

As we become conscious of His presence upon entering His Throne Room, our sins will come front and center in our minds. We will be like Isaiah saying, "Woe is me ... I am a man of unclean lips."[52] At that moment, we should instantly respond with

---

[50] Proverbs 28:13

[51] 1 John 1:6-9

[52] Isaiah 6:5

transparency and repentance. No covering. No blaming others. No excuses. No lying. Maturing in godliness is not a matter of sinless perfection, but immediate confession. God wants us to practice such confession as often as we sin. This transparency is designed to help us, not hurt us. God's intent is not for us to wallow in our sins, but to be released from sin's grip and trained in righteousness.

But there is more. In prayer, we will not only see how we have sinned against God but also see any unforgiveness we are carrying towards others. God wants us to forgive them just as we have been forgiven in order to show the world what it means when a believer walks with God. He wants us to represent Him well.

If someone hurt one of your children, you would have a hard time having a casual conversation with them until they had acknowledged and sought forgiveness for what they'd done. When we hurt God's children, He wants us to acknowledge, confess, and make restitution with those we've hurt. His great desire is unity in His family, which is one of the most profound witnesses the church has before a watching world. In fact, Jesus instructs us to stop our worship before Him until we have cleared our conscience.

> *"Therefore if you are presenting your offering at the altar, and there remember that your brother has something against you, leave your offering there before the altar and go; first be reconciled to your brother, and then come and present your offering.*[53]

God deeply transformed my life when I was 17 years old. I was a

---

[53] Matthew 5:23-24

believer but had wandered from the Lord for several years. God brought me to the end of myself and I finally surrendered my life completely back to Him. During that season, my father wisely advised me to take a legal pad, ask God to show me any sins I had committed against Him or others, and then write them down. I filled seven pages, front and back! I then went to those I had wronged and sought their forgiveness. I didn't have to be elaborate. My simple confession to them was this: "I'm trying to get my life right with God. He has shown me that what I did was wrong. Would you forgive me?" There wasn't a single person who denied that request.

I can remember the last phone call I made to clear my conscience. Finally, I knew that there was nothing between me and God or anyone else. The roof was off and the walls were down … and I was free! That was 50 years ago. I still make "sin lists" regularly. Thankfully they're not as long, but it is in this Spirit-evaluation that God continues to uncover needed areas of growth. And, I will need to do this until I die.

As you are praying, take deliberate time to let God examine your heart and then deal with all He discloses. Pray the prayer of David: *"Search me, O God, and know my heart; try me and know my anxious thoughts and see if there be any hurtful way in me, and lead me in the everlasting way."*[54]

---

[54] Psalm 139:23–24

ASSESSMENT

Where do I need further cleansing or
spiritual refinement today?

Prayer Movement 5: ARMOR

> *"And do not lead us into temptation, but deliver us from*
> *evil"*[55]

All of us deal with temptation daily. Temptation is not sin. We know this because Jesus was "tempted in all things as we are, yet without sin."[56] James gives us a definition of temptation.

> *But each one is tempted when he is carried away and*
> *enticed by his own lust. Then when lust has conceived, it*
> *gives birth to sin; and when sin is accomplished, it brings*
> *forth death.*[57]

We think of the Biblical word "lust" as an immoral desire. But the word is amoral. It gets its meaning by its context in a sentence. "Lust" simply means "strong desire." Everyone has natural desires (lusts) that are essential for life. We have a desire for food, for rest, for work, for sex, for achievement, for relationships. There is

---

[55] Matthew 6:13
[56] Hebrews 4:15
[57] James 1:14-15

nothing wrong with these desires. But the Enemy's scheme is to tempt us to fulfill legitimate desires in illegitimate ways.

For instance, it is right to fulfill our sexual desires with our mate in marriage. But Satan may tempt us to fulfill those desires with someone outside our marriage. If we are not wise, we will believe the Enemy's deceptions and reach out to indulge in that temptation. This is when lust "conceives" and "gives birth to sin."[58]

Like a fisherman who tempts a fish to fulfill his legitimate desire for food with a plastic bait, there is always a hook. When we take Satan's bait, it brings forth death—separation from the life of God.

One of our daily, hourly prayers should be "Lord, keep me from temptations that I cannot handle; temptations that are too strong for me—where I am particularly vulnerable. And deliver me from all evil and from the Evil One."

This is a preventative prayer. It is important to pray this for ourselves and also for those we love.

But when we are confronted by temptations, we can pray directly against the Enemy's onslaught. We often call these "Spiritual Warfare" prayers.

Imagine a high cliff. On top of the cliff is a plateau that represents the ground of our lives. It is subdivided into sections. One plot is our mental life; another our emotional life. One section of that land represents our financial life; another our relationships, and on and on. Every area of our life is represented.

Before we came to faith in Christ, Satan's flag was flying over that ground. We don't like to think about it, but Paul describes our lives before Christ in stark terms.

---

[58]James 1:14-15

And you were dead in your trespasses and sins, in which you formerly walked according to the course of this world, according to the prince of the power of the air, of the spirit that is now working in the sons of disobedience. Among them we too all formerly lived in the lusts of our flesh, indulging the desires of the flesh and of the mind, and were by nature children of wrath, even as the rest.[59]

When we came to Christ, we were transferred from "the kingdom of darkness into the kingdom of God's dear Son."[60] We surrendered our life to Christ and gave Him the title deed. The flag of Christ now flies over the land of our lives and Satan's ultimate rule is forever broken. We no longer belong to him.

But the Enemy does not give up easily. He comes crawling up the side of the cliff, peers over into our lives and says, "I want to take back some of this land so this believer will not be a strong witness for Christ. I know I can't own him anymore, but I'm going to tempt him to give up some ground to me so his life will not be a testimony to Christ." He begins his subtle deceptions and temptations. He tempts us to look to our possessions to give us life, or to fall into moral sin, or to be proud, or angry, or prayerless. If we are not wise, we take his bait and relinquish areas to his control.

But we don't have to be so naïve, and we are certainly not powerless. We have great power through Christ in prayer. "Greater is He that is in you than He that is in the world," John said.[61] And God has made a promise: "Resist the devil and he will flee from you."[62]

---

[59] Ephesians 2:1-3
[60] Colossians 1:13
[61] 1 John 4:4
[62] James 4:7

At the point of the devil's temptations, we must address him in prayer and remind him that the ground he is seeking to gain belongs to Jesus Christ. He's trespassing. We must remind the Enemy that Christ owns the title deed. We don't need to shout or use precise wording. We simply tell the Devil that he has no legal claim to any portion of our life. We resist him in prayer, commanding him to leave, and he must flee!

But don't be surprised if he comes back again, and again, and again. He tempted Jesus three times in a row. Finally, when he realized he could not get Jesus to take his bait, he left to return "at an opportune time."[63]

How do we deal with temptation? We pray unceasingly. We keep our eyes open to his temptations. We ask God to protect us and those we love from the Enemy's attacks and we deal with them in spiritual warfare praying when they come. We put on the full armor of God and pray. (We'll see more about this in the next chapter).

Millions of Christians before us have fought the Enemy and grown in Christlikeness through a praying life. Their lives have become a testimony to the greatness of the Owner.

ARMOR

Where do I need protection from temptation and evil today?

---

[63] Luke 4:13

Prayer Movement 6: ACKNOWLEDGEMENT

"For Yours is the kingdom, and the power, and the glory forever. Amen!"[64]

We have a problem. We've had it since the beginning. Every person thinks the world should revolve around them. That our lives are about our kingdom, our power, and our glory. The great agenda of God is to bring us back to His original design. He wants us to genuinely believe and continually acknowledge that the kingdom and the power and the glory belong to Him. This is not selfish of God; it is simply true. And He knows that our lives will be out of sync without this acknowledgment.

In heaven, this misunderstanding is eternally corrected. Notice the song of the saints and angels before God who see things perfectly.

> Then I looked, and I heard the voice of many angels around the throne and the living creatures and the elders; and the number of them was myriads of myriads, and thousands of thousands, saying with a loud voice, "Worthy is the Lamb that was slain to receive power and riches and wisdom and might and honor and glory and blessing." And every created thing which is in heaven and on the earth and under the earth and on the sea, and all things in them, I heard saying, "To Him who sits on the throne, and to the Lamb, be blessing and honor and glory and dominion for-

---

[64]Matthew 6:13

*ever and ever." And the four living creatures kept saying,
"Amen." And the elders fell down and worshiped.*[65]

The wise writer of Proverbs gives us instruction in this: "In all your ways acknowledge Him."[66] He is to be at the center of our minds and at the forefront of our confession. We are to let the world know that life is not just about us. It is about Him. Our days are to be spent in cooperating aggressively with God so His kingdom can come and His will be done on earth as it is in heaven.

This gets personal. I was miserable when I was running from the Lord as a young teenager. There's no one more unhappy than a disobedient Christian. I was living to establish my kingdom and receive glory and acknowledgment before others. My great goal was to be popular. God graciously brought me to the end of this self-centeredness and I finally, with joy, surrendered to His lordship. I acknowledged Him as the Lord of my life.

I wish that had been the only such acknowledgment that needed to occur, but my experience makes me know that this prayer must be prayed daily. I have had to repent thousands of times and reassert God on the throne of my life. A Christian must be a lifelong repenter. To write that statement grieves my heart, but it is true.

One of my greatest tests came years ago within our family. I became bitter towards God for a tragedy that had occurred in my parent's marriage. I couldn't believe God was allowing such a trial among people that loved Him. I didn't even know how deeply this bitterness had lodged in my heart.

---

[65] Revelation 5:11–14
[66] Proverbs 3:6

One night under a cottonwood tree in Norman, Oklahoma, I shook my fist (literally) at God. "If this is what it takes to make me a man of God (a prayer I'd often prayed), then I don't want it!" God in His grace began to gently, but strongly remind me that He was not the author of evil. He was the One who works all things together for good. He reminded me that I was holding at arm's length the only One who could help me through this trial.

I've often said that, at that moment, it was as if I had my fists clenched saying to God, "I will not accept this in my life," (which was foolish because it was already in my life!). But as God melted my heart under that tree, I relaxed my hands. I told the Lord in brokenness that I would accept this circumstance and embrace His sovereignty over my life. He had a right to do with my life whatever He desired. I acknowledged His Lordship. It was about His kingdom, His power, and His glory. The bitterness left and my soul was flooded with release and peace.

We will never find rest and usefulness until we acknowledge His Lordship. This is why Jesus included this final movement in His model prayer. When we have prayed for everything that God directs, we must come to this humble benediction:

"For Yours is the kingdom and the power and the glory forever. Amen!"

ACKNOWLEDGEMENT

Where do I need to acknowledge His Lordship in my life today?

Jesus took twelve men and taught them how to pray. They

came from different backgrounds, education, and experiences. They all had different giftings and abilities. But He knew they would not be effective if they did not learn how to live in unceasing communion with the Father. This was how He lived while on earth and it was how they must live. And then He used them to change the world!

Because of His gracious instruction, everyone—just like the apostles—can learn how to pray! Prayer can move from a duty to joy; from ineffectiveness to effective, fervent prayers that accomplish much; from routine experiences to the most important communion of our lives.

I had a simple, godly older man in my first church who knew how to commune with God. In his slow, Arkansas drawl, every prayer he prayed began with these words, *"Lord, thank You for the priv-e-lege of prayer!"*

I couldn't agree more.

CHAPTER 4

WHEN SHOULD WE PRAY?

GOD IS SPECIFIC. He leaves nothing to chance. When we ask the question, "When should I pray?" the answer comes instantly from His mouth: "Pray without ceasing."[67]

But this is not most believers' experience in prayer. It is one of the reasons Paul takes the majority of a chapter in Ephesians to convince us of the need for unrelenting intercession—a running dialogue with God all day long. In one of the most compelling passages in the Bible, we are reminded of the enemy we face, the armor we must have, and the battlefield where we must engage. And, it is the daily, hourly battlefield of prayer.

WE HAVE AN UNCEASING ENEMY

Satan has done a masterful job flooding our minds with fake news about himself. He's orchestrated a media diversion by characterizing himself as a funny little character in a red suit with a forked tail. In reality, other than God, he is the strongest force on earth, endowed with incredible powers. He is 100% evil and completely devoted to the destruction of God's kingdom.

---

[67] 1 Thessalonians 5:17

> *Finally, be strong in the Lord and in the strength of His might. Put on the full armor of God, so that you will be able to stand firm against the schemes of the devil. For our struggle is not against flesh and blood, but against the rulers, against the powers, against the world forces of this darkness, against the spiritual forces of wickedness in the heavenly places. Therefore, take up the full armor of God, so that you will be able to resist in the evil day, and having done everything, to stand firm.*[68]

He Has Powerful, though Temporary Authority

The words God uses are not random. We are fighting against powers, world forces of this darkness, spiritual forces of wickedness in heavenly places. Read back through this and think deeply about what this means. It implies that The Devil's forces are stronger than any mere human. He is orchestrating movements on earth. Impacting nations. Killing children. Destroying lives. And it is all driven by unadulterated wickedness.

He Has Schemes Designed to Make Us Fall

The word for "schemes" in the Greek language is "methodia." Satan has methods, wiles, strategies. He has specific plans for you, for your mate and children, and for your church and this world. This is not left to chance with Satan. He has a database that is more detailed than any on earth. He knows the exact, deceptive darts to throw at the exact right times, perfectly designed to bring destruction to our lives.

---

[68] Ephesians 6:10-13

One day as I was praying through this passage, I realized a sobering thing. I have 20 grandchildren (at last count!). The Enemy has schemes against my grandchildren! I must realize this and pick up the God-ordained weapons to combat these. I must ask God in prayer to reveal to me the methods the enemy has planned to use against my life, my family, my church, and my world. And then I should pray accordingly.

He Has an Evil Environment in Which to Work

We live in an "evil day." The "walls are down, and the gates are burned with fire" as Nehemiah said.[69] Satan has a far greater opportunity today to advance his cause than ever before.

Here's one illustration. The rise of media capabilities has exploded the possibilities for pornography and immorality. I could write some statistics here, but they would be out of date by the time this book is read. It seems an unstoppable force. Satan has obtained the high ground in the battle, at least in human terms, and there is little to stop his advance.

The sin of abortion is so commonplace that it is accepted and practiced by millions around the world. Satan has opened an unbelievably destructive door, killing millions of children.

Recently I was watching a news program in which government officials were promoting the most godless ideas possible. But what was so amazing was that they felt they were on legitimate moral ground. They reasoned that these things were good and helpful for people.

---

[69] Nehemiah 1:3

Such thinking springs from what God describes as a "reprobate mind" spoken of in Romans 1:28. The word "reprobate" means "unqualified; tested and found unworthy." It describes what happens when a person repeatedly ignores God and God finally gives them over to their own depraved thinking. He removes His restraining hand. Left to their own devices, a person completely loses the ability to distinguish right from wrong; to make proper moral judgments. Wrong IS right to them and vice-versa. The worst types of perversion begin to occur, but to the reprobate mind, they seem natural and right.

In years past, I occasionally heard this type of perverse thinking in our nation. Now, it seems to be the constant tone of the conversation.

What can protect us from this world? But, more importantly, what can penetrate this world in this evil day?

WE HAVE AN UNCEASING STRUGGLE

Because of the enemies we face and the world in which we live, the battle is incessant and intense. "For our STRUGGLE," Paul says. It is a word used in the Roman world describing intense, hand-to-hand combat.

And, it is "OUR struggle." No one is immune. No one is excepted. You may think that you are not facing such a battle. If so, it is a clear indication that Satan's deceptions have won the day in your thinking: that you think little of your Enemy and you think he thinks little of you. But if you are a true Christian, you are the temple of the Holy Spirit. The power of God is in you!

And "greater is He that is in you than he that is in the world".[70] Although you may not be aware of this fact, Satan is, and he knows that he must try with all his devices to put you on the spiritual sidelines so God's power can be limited through you. He wants to extinguish the light.

One of my sons, David, was a missionary for several years in Phnom Penh, Cambodia. Early on he noticed an unusual number of children with no arms or legs. Upon investigation, he discovered that land mines had been left in the fields following the Viet Nam War. Children would wander into the fields to play and the results were horrific.

If you don't realize you're on the Enemy's battlefield you could become a casualty of war, even though you thought you were just going out for an afternoon stroll. This is why Paul reminds us of our battlefield weapons. There are things we must do to win this battle.

Be Strong in the Lord

Be strong in the Lord and the strength of His might.[71]

Paul realizes our human limitations. We do not have the resources to overcome this spiritual enemy. Therefore we must find our strength "in the Lord and the strength of His might." This means we must realize our need constantly and cry out for God to fill us with Himself. We must trust in His strength.

One weekend I became very sick. I was up all Saturday night and had to preach a very intense message the next morning. I

---

[70] 1 John 4:4
[71] Ephesians 6:10

felt, after prayer, that I must preach and not call on someone else, even though I had not had one moment of sleep.

The next morning, I was praying before the service.

"Lord, I don't think I have the strength to preach these services," I said.

"Who said this was about your strength?" God said.

"Lord, would You be my strength this morning?" I humbly asked.

"Of course I will. It's what I've always wanted to do," He replied.

By God's grace, I went out and preached with power (and collapsed at home that afternoon!) The realization that you don't have the necessary power to prevail against the Enemy means that you must pray without ceasing, relying on God's strength, particularly as you face spiritual battles.

Be Clothed in His Armor

> Put on the full armor of God so that you will be able to
> stand firm against the schemes of the devil.[72]

This image was clear to the hearers in Paul's day as they observed the Roman soldiers that filled every town. Using that image of war, Paul reminds us of the necessity for the believer to clothe himself with spiritual armor in battle—armor which is available to every Christian. It is wise at the beginning of each day to "put on" your armor in prayer.

---

[72]Ephesians 6:11

- GIRD YOUR LOINS WITH TRUTH. This means truthfulness, honesty, integrity which will protect us from the temptations to the opposite which would make us vulnerable. It also implies knowing and believing the truth that will guard us against the lies of the father of all lies, Satan.

- PUT ON THE BREASTPLATE OF RIGHTEOUSNESS. We must realize and claim the righteousness we have in Christ and also cover our vital organs with a commitment to personal holiness.

- SHOD YOUR FEET WITH THE PREPARATION OF THE GOSPEL OF PEACE. We must get ready to move by realizing our calling. We lace up our witnessing shoes. We must prepare to share the gospel of peace gladly and quickly with everyone we meet, which is Satan's greatest fear.

- TAKE UP THE SHIELD OF FAITH WHICH CAN QUENCH ALL THE FLAMING ARROWS OF THE WICKED ONE. One of the most powerful weapons in battle was a flaming arrow. The Romans had developed a defensive weapon in a body-sized, leather shield. It had a front and a back with a vacuum between which would quench a flaming arrow. Satan is continually flinging darts at us designed to destroy us. We often think these are just our thoughts. But I'm convinced otherwise. Our powerful defense is faith, and "faith comes by hearing and hearing by the Word of Christ."[73] We must combat his flaming arrows with the faith that comes from God's Word.

---

[73] Romans 10:17

- TAKE UP THE HELMET OF SALVATION. That which protects us most in our battle is our absolute security in Christ if we have come to know Him. Our salvation saves us in our minds. We must remember this as we face the day.

- TAKE UP THE SWORD OF THE SPIRIT WHICH IS THE WORD OF GOD. There is nothing more powerful than Scripture. It is God's Word and our greatest weapon against Satan's lies. Jesus Himself rebuked every temptation of the Enemy in the wilderness with God's Word, and so must we. This is why Scripture memory is so vital.

It is a critical exercise each day, and multiple times throughout the day, to check our strength (making sure we're relying on the Lord) and check our armor (using the right protective weapons against the Enemy).

Thus armed, how do we fight the battle? Where is the battle against this enemy won? Paul's answer is surprising to most Christians.

Be Unceasing in Prayer!

With all prayer and petition pray at all times in the Spirit, and with this in view, be on the alert with all perseverance and petition for all the saints.[74]

This is where the battle is won or lost! We are to "stand firm." But then we are to penetrate the Enemy's territory with unceasing prayer. Notice the four "alls" in this verse.

---

[74]Ephesians 6:18

- "ALL PRAYER AND PETITION"— We must use the arsenal of prayer that Jesus taught us in Matthew 6: adoration, alignment, access, assessment, armor, acknowledgment. We must employ every type of prayer that is at our disposal, applying them as needed.

- "ALL TIMES IN THE SPIRIT"— There is never a moment, a thought, a decision, a circumstance that we should not instantly address in prayer. And, it should be prayer "in the Spirit." In other words, we must be tuned to the Holy Spirit, letting Him initiate prayers through us. Powerful prayer is a loop that begins with God, passes through us, and ascends to the throne. And God-initiated prayer is always effective!

- "ALL PERSEVERANCE"— We must never give up. Like the persevering widow in Luke 18, we must cry out day and night until the battle is won. Many battles are lost simply because we abandoned the field too soon. As we are convinced of God's promises, we pray continuously until the promises are realized.

- "FOR ALL THE SAINTS"— One of the noblest practices of the United States military is that they seek to never leave a soldier on the field. The strength of the military is their willingness to help each other. When soldiers develop a camp, they place soldiers around the perimeter to protect. Each guard scans the field to their right and left, covering their comrades.

Every believer we know needs our prayers and we need theirs! They are in the midst of the battle with us. We don't want the Enemy to slip into our camp simply because we are not providing covering prayer to those in the battle with us. We must pray for the spiritual leaders who are on the front lines, but also for every spiritual warrior.

And, we must remember why we are in this battle—why we should pray so fervently and unceasingly ...

WE HAVE AN UNCEASING MISSION!

There is no mystery about our mission. Whether we realize it or not, engage in it or not, we have one mission, for which Paul requested prayer.

> *"Pray on my behalf, that utterance may be given to me in the opening of my mouth, to make known with boldness the mystery of the gospel, for which I am an ambassador in chains; that in proclaiming it I may speak boldly, as I ought to speak."*[75]

Prayer is not merely about getting a few things for ourselves or simply being helped when we are in trouble. It's about advancing the kingdom of God! It is God's weapon to invade Enemy territory and snatch people from the jaws of Satan who has come to "steal, kill, and destroy."[76]

It is telling that almost every prayer Paul requested from others was for boldness to proclaim the gospel. Not for health, wealth, or prosperity. Not even for safety. Paul asked them to pray that he

---

[75]Ephesians 6:19
[76]John 10:10

would open his mouth and boldly proclaim the gospel. He needed their prayers for mission-driven courage.

There are millions of people who are enslaved to the Enemy. We have the singular message that can release them from his clutches. They cannot be delivered unless we pierce through the Enemy lines and get the life-saving message to them. And prayer is the power that makes all of this work!

> Up in a little town in Maine, things were pretty dead some years ago. The churches were not accomplishing anything. There were a few Godly men in the churches, and they said: 'Here we are, only uneducated laymen; but something must be done in this town. Let us form a praying band. We will all center our prayers on one man. Who shall it be?'
>
> They picked out one of the hardest men in town, and centered all their prayers upon him. In a week, he was converted. They centered their prayers upon the next hardest man in town, and soon he was converted. Then they took up another and another until within a year, over two hundred people were brought to God, and the fire spread out into all the surrounding country. Definite prayer for those in the prison house of sin is the need of the hour.[77]

When do lost people need to hear the gospel? All the time, every day. When do Christians need boldness to share the gospel? All

---

[77] R. A. Torrey, *How to Pray*

the time, every day. When should we be praying for the fulfillment of God's mission through us? All the time, every day.

CHAPTER 5

WHAT IS EXTRAORDINARY PRAYER?

EVERYONE FACES EMERGENCIES IN LIFE. We face financial problems, diseases, accidents, family difficulties. Such times call for immediate, deliberate adjustments in our priorities and schedules.

Sometimes these emergencies affect whole nations. At such times in America, the governmental leaders have the option to declare a National State of Emergency. Such an emergency has been described as ...

> "A governmental declaration which usually suspends some normal functions of executive, legislative and judicial powers, alerts citizens to change their normal behaviors, or orders government agencies to implement emergency preparedness plans."[78]

We have faced several of these in our nation's history. The bombing of the Twin Towers in New York on September 11, 2001, led the United States President to declare a National State of Emergency regarding terrorism that is in effect as I write. Vast changes were made to bring greater security.

---

[78] Courses.Lumenlearning.com

The spring of 2020 ushered in an amazing event. A microcosmic virus swept across nations and shut down the world in a matter of months. Every nation suspended normal functions, alerted citizens to change their normal behaviors, and implemented emergency plans.

As God looks at the state of our nation, we must think deeply about His evaluation of our land. If Scripture is any indication, He would tell us that we are in a National *Spiritual* Emergency. So what should we do? Simply go on with business as usual? Or should we agree about the nature of this dramatic problem, change our normal behaviors, and implement emergency plans?

EXTRAORDINARY MOVEMENTS

Throughout history, God has chosen seasons to "rend the heavens and come down."[79] These times of revival in the church and massive spiritual awakening among the lost are used by God to remind us of what heaven is like and to make His kingdom come on earth as it is in heaven. It is His great mercy that brings such times. When the church and a nation sink to desperate spiritual lows, the cry of our hearts should be for such revivals and awakenings.

Richard Owen Roberts describes revival as "The extraordinary movement of the Spirit of God among His people that produces extraordinary results."[80] God is at work everywhere all the time. But seasons of revival accelerate the movement of God, accomplishing in a matter of days or months what could not be accomplished in decades.

---

[79] Isaiah 64:1
[80] Richard Owen Roberts, *Revival*

Revives the Church

Revival brings the church to life again. In 1857 a noon-day prayer meeting began with six men led by Jeremiah Lanphier. They must have assumed in its beginning that it was just another normal prayer meeting by a few earnest believers. But God had other plans. No one could explain what happened in the succeeding weeks. Soon 50,000 people were gathering daily to pray in New York City! This is the church revived! Such acceleration in prayer does not merely lead to revival, it IS revival, as Jonathan Edwards said.

Revival, above everything else glorifies Christ. It restores Him to the center of each believer's life and the life of the Church. It creates an intense passion for Christ, fueled by the atmosphere of His presence. And it revives the church to her ultimate mission.

Awakens the Lost

There have been five nationwide seasons of extraordinary revival and spiritual harvest in America to date. Historians debate the dates and the extent of each has varied.

- The First Great Awakening 1735-1742

- The Second Great Awakening 1800-1825

- The Prayer Revival 1857-1858

- The Welsh Revival 1904-1905

- The Jesus Movement 1969-1971

Notice that every 50-60 years in our history God has graciously come in power to our nation bringing the course correction that we desperately need.

The telling mark of these movements has not been just the change in the churches, but the rapid expansion of the gospel. Awakening implies that a man is in spiritual slumber, unable to find God. God in His grace quickens his heart, bringing him to an awareness of his sin, a deep desire for repentance, and faith to believe in Christ. In times of national spiritual awakening, this happens with stunning speed.

In the First Great Awakening, 15% of the population was saved. Do the math for your city or state and you will see the massive nature of such a movement. During the height of the 1857 Prayer Revival, it was reported that 20,000 people a week were coming to faith in Christ! In the Welsh Revival, 100,000 people experienced salvation in nine months, fulfilling the vision God had given to Evan Roberts in prayer, and this happened in a country that is the size of a small American state. That Awakening swept around the world, dramatically affecting America as well.

Records of the largest denomination of its time, the Southern Baptist Convention in America, show that more students and teenagers were baptized in 1969-1971 than any moment in that denomination's history—before or since. This was during the Jesus Movement.

Samuel Davies was the President of Princeton and known as the "Apostle of Virginia." He said that before the first Great Awakening humble pastors preached with little results. When the revival came, he said that they would preach the same messages and hundreds of people would be saved. His observation was that "the gospel became almighty and carried everything before it."[81] If you long for millions to be saved, pray for a nationwide, spiritual awakening.

Transforms the Culture

Such dramatic invasions by God alter the culture. The pastor of Saint John's-Wood Presbyterian Church declared after the Welsh Revival that "the mighty unseen breath of the Spirit was doing in a month more than centuries of legislation could accomplish."[82] Samuel Davies also said, "There are eras when only a large outpouring of the Spirit can produce a public general reformation."[83]

The Welsh Revival is full of accounts of such public transformation. Drunkenness, immorality, and crimes of every nature were brought to nothing. With all our best efforts in America, the tides of immorality, abortion, and family breakups are not subsiding. Only a nationwide revival would produce such effects.

Accelerates the Mission

If you love the cause of world missions, you should pray for revival. When God revives His people, their hearts begin to beat in sync with Him who came to "seek and save that which is lost."[84] A quick study will reveal that every major mission movement in history came out of the fires of revival.

The mission advance with Count von Zinzendorf and the Moravians began with the Moravian Pentecost, igniting a prayer meet-

---

[81]Ian Murray, *Revival and Revivalism*
[82]Ibid
[83]Ibid
[84]Luke 19:10

ing that lasted 100 years and sent missionaries around the world in a day when this was unheard of. Most Moravian missionaries left with their goods packed in a coffin, vowing to give their lives on the field for the cause.

The modern missions movement with William Carey and the Haystack Prayer meeting in America both occurred in the early 1800s in the fever-heat of the Second Great Awakening. Hudson Taylor, George Mueller, and William Booth were all men touched by extraordinary movements in their nations. If we love missions, we must pray for revival!

EXTRAORDINARY PRAYER

We cannot manipulate God to send such movements, but we are charged by God to unite our hearts in repentant prayer for spiritual awakenings. There is a clear cycle in the Bible and human history. As the church declines, God sends His disciplining judgments. This is the mercy of God.

Like pain to the human body, this is remedial and intended to wake us up and bring us back to Him. When we get desperate enough, we begin to cry out to God in united, fervent prayer. And there is something uniquely irresistible to God about a united cry. In answer to this cry (orchestrated by God Himself), He hears and answers, sending the revival and awakening we need.

Jonathan Edwards was perhaps the greatest theologian America has ever produced. He was a brilliant but also deeply spiritual and passionate pastor and leader. He is the principal name associated with the First Great Awakening that began around 1735. He stood in the revival fire of God's movement in which 15% of the nation came to faith in Christ.

When the revival began to wane, Edwards wrote a small, but vitally important book in 1746. This book framed much of the religious thinking in America for the next 100 years. The title is telling, as was often the case in his day.

> *A Humble Attempt to Promote Explicit Agreement and Visible Union Among God's People in Extraordinary Prayer for the Revival of Religion and the Advancement of Christ's Kingdom on Earth, Pursuant to Scripture-Promises and Prophecies Concerning the Last Time*

The great revival historian, J. Edwin Orr, said that to read the title was to have read the book! Each word must have been chosen with prayerful precision by Edwards and is worth examination, particularly since they were written by such a great theologian who had experienced a nationwide revival in his day.

A Humble Attempt to Promote

Edwards was seeing the wane of revival fires. His book was an attempt (just like this book) to awaken people to what was happening—the spiritual emergency—and rouse them to action.

Explicit Agreement

One man might say, "This is the problem in our nation," while another cries, "No, it is something else." Edwards believed that to ignite a movement that would move the heart of God, there must be agreement about the problem and solution. Edwards believed the problem was (and is today) that people had forgotten God and wandered from Him. And the solution was an outpouring of revival and awakening.

And Visible Union

Edwards knew that something extraordinary happens when people are united. Throughout the Bible there are multiple phrases or its equivalent like this: "And all the people cried out." Each time there was such desperation that led to a united cry, God heard and answered. A.T. Pierson was right when he said, "There has never been a spiritual awakening in any country or locality that did not begin in united prayer."

Among God's People

It is to His children that God directs the commands to pray for revival, for only these understand and are spiritually capable to do so. This is why the great promise of 2 Chronicles 7:14 begins with a conditional phrase:

> If My people who are called by My name humble them-selves and pray and seek My face and turn from their wicked ways, then I will hear from heaven, will forgive their sin, and will heal their land.

In Extraordinary Prayer for the Revival of Religion and the Advancement of Christ's Kingdom on Earth

What were the means that Edwards believed would usher in revival and awakening? Was it a fresh program? A new or novel idea? A united campaign? A catchy method? What does God call for in times of national, spiritual emergency? Edwards knew through Biblical understanding and practical experience that there was one thing we must do: We must pray and pray in an extraordinary way.

If we long for revival and awakening and understand that it is the great need of the hour, then what kind of praying should we do? What did Edwards mean when he called for "extraordinary prayer?"

MORE Prayer

The praying that you are doing is ordinary prayer to you. Desperate times call for desperate prayer. More prayer is needed. More intensity. More time. More people praying.

We do not manipulate God by our praying, but there are some things that God plans to accomplish through prayer that He will not do any other way. Why else would God invite us to pray and make such promises about its effectiveness? Why would He tell us that we "do not have because we do not ask?"[85] God is training us to rule and reign with Him eternally, and our training begins now. He has planned to involve us deeply in His redemptive work.

I have often heard people say, "I don't think it matters how much or how long you pray." These are often people who pray little and reap little. A wonderful goal would be to see our prayer life increase in its time and intensity every year.

Some prayer, some power. More prayer, more power. Much prayer, much power.

---

[85] James 4:2

FOUNDATIONAL Prayer

If someone gave you money to build a home, you would develop your plans with an architect. But you might discover that the money they provided was not enough. Back to the architect you'd go. You would downsize one room or another, maybe even deciding that some rooms would be nice, but unnecessary. But there is one part of the construction you could not eliminate: the foundation. Even though unseen, everything depends on a solid foundation.

Most churches have multiple components. There is the worship ministry, the preaching ministry, the children and student ministry, the missions ministry. Off to the side—peripheral at best—is the prayer ministry. It is small and even non-existent in most churches and a sign of our urgent need for revival. It illustrates a foundational conviction we must embrace:

Prayer is not a side-room … *it is the foundation!*

Study the Scripture and see if this is not so. Read the 650 passages on prayer in your 1,000-page Bible and determine where prayer should fit into your life and your church. Pick up any biography of a great Christian leader and you will instantly see that prayer was never peripheral. They lived and moved in unceasing prayer, and it was the primary secret of their power with God and man.

PERSEVERING Prayer

There is a reason that Jesus taught us we must "pray at all times and not lose heart."[86] We have a great adversary that seeks to

---

[86] Luke 18:1

distract us from prayer, knowing it is our most powerful weapon. We are weak in our flesh and can easily give up. But we must "ask and keep on asking" if we are to receive. The unrighteous judge in Jesus' parable was moved by the widow's unceasing requests, and God is moved by our persevering prayer.

> Prayer is warfare. It is a fiercely contested conflict. The enemy yields only what he must. He yields only what is taken. Therefore the ground must be taken step by step. Prayer must be definite. He yields only when he must. Therefore, prayer must be persistent. He continually renews his attacks, therefore the ground must be held against him in the Savior's name.[87]

DESPERATE Prayer

If you had a daughter and you were asked to pray for her you might pray something like this: "Lord, thank You for my daughter. Keep her safe. Provide for her needs. Help her find the path of life." This would be a great prayer—the kind of prayer we should pray constantly for our children.

But what if your daughter went on a mission trip and, through a strange set of events, she was abducted by terrorists. You tried desperately to find her to no avail. And you discovered that she was being terribly abused. If you were then asked to pray for your daughter, how would you pray? You would pray desperately.

We fail to realize in our nation what is happening to the Bride of Christ; how she is being attacked; what is being done to the

---
[87] S.D. Gordon, *Quiet Talks on Prayer*

name of Christ. Enjoying our conveniences, we lose sight of the battlefield and the mission. We forget that we are frontline troops enlisted to engage the Enemy and advance God's kingdom. We are to live to snatch men and women, boys and girls from the clutches of the Great Terrorist who wants to see them in hell eternally.

Leonard Ravenhill said, "The reason we don't have revival is that we are willing to live without it." The intensity of our prayers for revival will always relate to the depth of our desperation, the height of our love for God's glory, and the breadth of our passion for those far from Him. Such desperation drives us to action.

> And in movements of the Spirit the first thing that happens and which eventually leads to a great revival is that one man or a group of men suddenly begin to feel this burden and they feel the burden so much that they are led to do something about it.[88]

Would you pause right now and ask God to burn the need in your heart so that it would forever burden you for revival and spiritual awakening? Ask Him to create a desperation in your heart and the hearts of each of us that would drive us to *extraordinary prayer*.

---

[88] Martyn Lloyd-Jones, *Revival*

CHAPTER 6

HOW SHOULD WE PRAY
FOR REVIVAL AND AWAKENING?

IF YOU SEE SOMETHING WONDERFUL in kingdom life you should understand that there was always something previous. Looking at a newborn baby, you can be assured that there were nine months of "previous," as every new mother will tell you!

When you see a person come to faith in Christ you must realize that there were days, perhaps years of the Wind blowing across the surface of their heart and mind, bringing them to spiritual birth.

Just as this is true in our physical and spiritual lives, it is also true in the birth of movements of revival and spiritual awakening. God is always previous.

R. B. Jones was a pastor during the Welsh Revival of 1904-1905. Twenty years later, some were criticizing the revival, and Jones wrote a book to explain what really happened. In his wonderful book, *Rent Heavens,* he describes the previous work of God.

> Though every revival ultimately culminates in a form which attracts the attention of all, no revival is of sudden origin. Behind the startling outburst is a process

> which sometimes goes on for years, a purifying and
> preparatory process. It was so in connection with
> that of 1904.[89]

If we are going to pray for and cooperate with God in revival, we need to understand His ways—what He is doing—and join Him. Revival, in its simplest terms, could be described with one word: GOD! It is God manifested; God restored to His rightful place in the earth; God moving with accelerated speed; God rending the heavens and coming down.

The greatest manifestation of God was seen in the coming of Christ as "the Word became flesh and dwelt among us and we saw His glory."[90] If you will study Luke 3:1-18, and the parallel passages in the Gospels, you will see God prepared the world for this manifestation of His glory. It is pictured for us in the work of John the Baptist.

A study of revival history will illustrate that the elements present in John's work are generally what has preceded most nationwide movements of revival and awakening.

GOD'S PREPARATORY WORK

God did things in the days of John the Baptist—and through John the Baptist—that paved the way and prepared hearts for Christ's coming. In fact, John quoted Isaiah's great prophecy to describe what was happening. These are things we must pray for if we are to join God in His work of revival.

---

[89] R. B. Jones, *Rent Heavens: Some of It's Hidden Springs and Prominent Results*
[90] John 1:14

As it is written in the book of the words of Isaiah the prophet,
"THE VOICE OF ONE CRYING IN THE WILDERNESS,
'MAKE READY THE WAY OF THE LORD,
MAKE HIS PATHS STRAIGHT. EVERY RAVINE WILL BE FILLED,
AND EVERY MOUNTAIN AND HILL WILL BE BROUGHT LOW;
THE CROOKED WILL BECOME STRAIGHT,
AND THE ROUGH ROADS SMOOTH;
AND ALL FLESH WILL SEE THE SALVATION OF GOD.' "[91]

Voices Are Sent

*There came **a man sent from God**, whose name was John.*[92]

John was not sent from a committee or a church or a group of like-minded zealots. He was sent from God. When God prepares His people for His coming, He raises up both new and old voices.

And what was John to do? John the Baptist tells us ...

*"**I am a voice** of one crying in the wilderness."*[93]

John saw himself not as a Messiah, or an organizer, or an event planner, but merely a voice preparing the way for the coming Messiah. He did not draw attention to himself or his ministry. He saw himself humbly and rightly as a channel for the message of God. When God prepares a nation for revival, humble voices are raised to speak God's truth.

And where did John get this message? How did He become this voice?

---

[91] Luke 3:4-6
[92] John 1:6 *(emphasis added)*
[93] John 1:23a *(emphasis added)*

*In the high priesthood of Annas and Caiaphas, **the word of God came to John,** the son of Zacharias, in the wilderness.*[94]

John had received the words and theme of his message from God. He was merely relaying what God had told him to announce. Notice this message had three primary components. It was a message of ...

- REPENTANCE: John announced that something was terribly wrong and there needed to be massive spiritual adjustments in people's lives. They needed to look for a Savior.

- JUDGMENT: John told them that if they did not repent, judgment would surely come.

- HOPE: John also promised that One was coming who would baptize them with fire and power!

When God prepares us for a new work of revival and awakening, we will begin to see voices rising, sent from God Himself. Voices proclaiming this same message of repentance, judgment, and hope.

Desperation Deepens and a Cry Erupts

As John preached, people became disturbed, convicted, and desperate for God. A spiritual expectation began to build and a cry lifted from almost every segment of the society—a cry for something different.

---

[94] Luke 3:2 *(emphasis added)*

*And the crowds were questioning him, saying, **"Then what shall we do?"***

*And some tax collectors also came to be baptized, and they said to him, **"Teacher, what shall we do?"***

*Some soldiers were questioning him, saying, "And what about us, **what shall we do?"** [95]*

Have you heard these questions lately? What is happening in our nation? What will bring change to the land? What has gone wrong? And, what should we do? If so, this is merely the work of God creating hunger.

God can use any means to create desperation. But such anxiety is the only thing that can push an entire nation towards God. When we get desperate enough, we cry out and God always answers a humble, united, repentant cry. We would be wise to see increasing turmoil in our nation as a sign that God is driving us to desperation, which could lead to spiritual awakening.

Repentance Is Restored

*And all the country of Judea was going out to him, and all the people of Jerusalem; and they were being baptized by him in the Jordan River, **confessing their sins.** [96]*

One of the clear marks of coming revival is a deeper and deeper recognition of personal sin. Notice Isaiah's response when he saw the Lord in Isaiah 6. His was a cry of repentance and confession.

---

[95] Luke 3:10-14 *(emphasis added)*
[96] Mark 1:5 *(emphasis added)*

The great revival promise in 2 Chronicles 7:14 does not say, "If my people will humble themselves and pray and seek My face and 'think badly about their sin' or, 'talk about the terrible condition of the government,' or, 'feel upset about what godless individuals are doing to the nation.'" It says, "If my people ... will TURN."

Would you pause and answer this question: Are you turning? Are you more convinced of your sin, more obedient to Christ, more repentant than you were a year ago? If we're not, we're not cooperating with God in His reviving work.

When revival fires begin, repentance begins.

Unity Builds

> And **all the country** of Judea was going out to him, and all the people of Jerusalem; and they were being baptized by him in the Jordan River.[97]

The Bible is literal. When it says "all" it means "all." In John's day, there was a widespread, unified interest in the things of God. Spiritual unity was growing.

In every instance of nationwide revival, we see God's people uniting all across the land. They will always maintain some of their differences—both doctrinal and practical—but they prioritize them so that they can unite on the main thing. They come together to cry out for God to manifest Himself in power, knowing it is their only hope.

Pray for such unity to occur. And, as you witness it, give thanks that revival may be coming soon. Don't let your preoccupation

---

[97] Mark 1:5 *(emphasis added)*

with secondary issues abort unity on the primary calling of united prayer.

Spiritual Activity Increases

Notice in Mark 1:5 that all the people were going out to hear John. Multitudes of people were being baptized and confessing their sins. The spiritual activity reached such a fever pitch that everyone noticed something unusual was happening.

In the ten years preceding the Welsh revival, pastors began to hold conventions to restore the teachings regarding revival and the work of the Holy Spirit. Somehow, they felt that these teachings had been lost and needed to be reasserted. Many were attending, prayer was increasing, spiritual activity grew. This was true in almost every Great Awakening in history. In fact, it is often hard to distinguish this preparatory season from the actual moments when revival and awakening are recognized.

Often, we speak of the catalytic moments we observe in history that signal revival, such as Jeremiah Lanphier's prayer meetings in 1857 or the preaching of Evan Roberts in the Welsh Revival. But, in reality, revival most often comes not as a solitary eruption, but a rising tide.

Christ Is Exalted!

> And he was preaching, and saying, "After me One is coming who is mightier than I, and I am not fit to stoop down and untie the thong of His sandals. I baptized you with water; but He will baptize you with the Holy Spirit."[98]

---

[98] Mark 1:7-8

It is important to notice that the message which preceded the coming of the manifest presence of Christ was not of revival ... it was a message pointing to Christ. John the Baptist's preaching exalted the only One who deserved to be pursued.

Revival preaching should be Christ-centric, not merely revival-centric. When Christ is exalted, we see our sin and need and the great answer we only find in Him. In the first Great Awakening, Jonathan Edwards was preaching to many people in the church who were unregenerate church members. His message was to preach Christ and Christ alone.

OUR PREPARATORY WORK

Do we see signs of God's preparatory work towards revival and awakening now? If so, then what should we be doing to pray and prepare for His coming? And how should we join God in His work?

Don't Swell Up!

"He must increase, but I must decrease."[99]

John understood his place, which was why he could be so greatly used. God may allow many people to be used by Him during days of revival and awakening, even some who are surprising to the established church. The quickest way to quench God's work and to assure that we will not be used in the process is to swell in pride and draw attention to ourselves. This can happen easily as God begins to accelerate His work and we vainly think it was because of our doing.

---

[99]John 3:30

The Jesus Movement of the 1970s was an extraordinary season. Tens of thousands of people came to Christ, particularly students. The "hippies" of that generation who had rebelled against parents and society were brought to Christ in record numbers. God began to use them with their long hair and guitars. But the great tragedy of that movement was that many churches did not recognize how God was using new people. Wanting to keep their old wineskins, they resisted God's work as He raised up new, young leaders. Most revival historians will agree that the movement was quenched far too quickly because of that resistance.

Don't be surprised at who God uses in revival. And, if He uses you, give Him all the glory.

Don't Give Up!

So with many other exhortations, he preached the gospel to the people.[100]

John accepted his assignment and we must accept ours. He was willing to pray and proclaim the gospel to the end, even when it cost him his life. We cannot give up praying for the manifest presence of Christ. When revival comes, it will come on the wings of the multiplied prayers of faithful people that have been prayed over decades. We must pray and proclaim and not faint.

In Little Rock, Arkansas, a praying band of women took the phone book of the city, divided it up, and prayed through it over and over again, crying out to God for revival. As of this writing, this prayer meeting has lasted for fifty years! Any measure of revival

---

[100]Luke 3:18

that comes to that city will trace its roots to a humble group of persistent intercessors.

Look Up!

This is the great reward of our cooperation with God in revival praying. Mark's account of John the Baptist's work goes straight to the glorious reward: *In those days Jesus came!*[101]

Imagine this moment. John the Baptist had gone into the wilderness and lived a barren lifestyle. He cared for nothing but his task to prepare the way for the Coming One. He was ridiculed and mocked. Many turned away. Perhaps he wondered what was happening and if what he was doing was right.

But one glorious day he looked up and saw the One he had been preparing for. The answer to every prayer. The theme of every message. And seeing Him he said, *"Behold the Lamb of God who takes away the sin of the world!"*[102] And nothing was ever the same. His manifest presence changed everything.

Our prayers for the continued manifestations of Christ in revival and awakening are worth it! We could pray for decades for needed revival and even if we did not see it in our day those prayers would not be wasted. Great Awakenings have always been preceded by extraordinary prayer. To witness such Divine moments is to peer into heaven, for heaven comes to earth. Christ manifests Himself, and the glorious results of that awakening redeems millions.

---

[101] Mark 1:9
[102] John 1:29

As you pray for such outpourings, perhaps this understanding of God's preparatory work could frame your intercession.

Dear Reviving God,
*please **SEND VOICES** that will speak what the world needs to hear—*
a message of repentance and judgment and hope.
*Let **DESPERATION GROW** so deeply that a **CRY WILL ERUPT***
among your people.
*May we turn in genuine **REPENTANCE** and humbly come back to You.*
*May **UNITY BUILD** and **SPIRITUAL ACTIVITY INCREASE***
like a rising tide.
*Help us to exalt **CHRIST** and Christ alone in our proclaiming and*
praying,
*And then, Lord Jesus, **COME** in power,*
reviving Your church and sweeping millions into Your kingdom!

CHAPTER 7

WHAT HINDERS PRAYER?

IT WAS A BRIGHT, SPRING DAY when my neighborhood friend invited me to work with him on his car. I was happy to join him. But there was just one problem: at the ripe old age of twelve, I knew nothing about cars. Nothing! He told me to start taking the engine apart, and we would put it back together later. I did, he did, and his engine parts lay in his front yard for the next six months! I'm sure everybody in the neighborhood really appreciated this spectacle. We worked very hard, but our work was worse than useless. It merely created a junkyard on a nice street!

Most believers are getting desperate. What we are doing in the church is not producing the desired results. As we look at the world around us—the moral and spiritual free-fall that is occurring and the declining condition of the church in our land—we are driven to cry out to God. We need Him. We need His manifest presence. We need revival in the church and spiritual awakening among the unbelieving. We need our nation to be restored to its kingdom calling as a mighty, gospel-sending station to the world.

As you study the scripture, you realize that the precursor to any great movement of God is always humble, repentant prayer. Many people across the country are praying in record numbers.

But wouldn't it be tragic to discover that our prayers are not being effective? That they are not being regarded by God? That there are things in our lives that are hindering our prayers from accomplishing what is so desperately needed? That, for all our hard work in prayer, it is doing nothing to advance the kingdom? That we are simply littering heaven's yard with unusable prayers?

GOD'S NEGATIVE PROMISES

While there are hundreds of positive promises regarding answered prayer, there are also some places in Scripture where God outlines what will hinder our prayers. No one prays perfectly and God is not playing with us. He does not make intercession so unattainable that only the mature can be effective. He knows our frame and understands our weakness. But He is also very clear about those things that can hinder our prayers.

Would you be willing to evaluate the effectiveness of your prayer life? Step-by-step, walk through the following questions with an honest heart. If God shows you areas of need, turn to Him in repentance and take every step necessary to adjust your life to encounter Him afresh in prayer.

SOME PRAYER-HINDERING QUESTIONS

1. Are you simply praying?

"You do not have because you do not ask."[103]

Many people do not receive answers from their prayers because they do not pray. They talk about prayer, teach and preach about

---

[103]James 4:3c

prayer, tell people "I'm praying for you!" but it is often hypocrisy. You may not be seeing God's activity in and through your life because you have not taken the steps to become a man or woman who is simply praying.

2. Are you praying simply?

> "And when you are praying, do not use meaningless repetition as the Gentiles do, for they suppose that they will be heard for their many words. So do not be like them; for your Father knows what you need before you ask Him."[104]

God is not impressed by flowery words or fine oratory. He loves sincere, simple hearts. He knows our needs and is not waiting for us to petition Him with perfect elocution. He wants us! He longs for His children to climb up in His lap and enjoy Him.

One of the most liberating experiences in prayer is to realize you can come to Him in sincerity, honesty, and simplicity, speaking to Him as a friend to a friend or a child to a loving Father.

3. Are you entering in?

> "But you, when you pray, go into your inner room, close your door and pray to your Father who is in secret, and your Father who sees what is done in secret will reward you."[105]

"Hurry is the death of prayer," said Samuel Chadwick. Many have not learned how to enter into God's presence. If you were to enter

---

[104] Matthew 6:7-8
[105] Matthew 6:6

physically into His presence, you would not pop in, read a list of requests, and pop out. You would quiet your soul. You would be humbled by His magnificence. You would worship and adore Him. You would "hallow" His name.

You can enter into the closet of prayer anywhere—in a room with a few friends or a congregation of thousands. But you *must* enter in and shut the door on the outside and turn your gaze to the Father. Only then will you begin to find yourself in a posture to hear from Him. And only as you hear from Him are you able to pray fervent prayers that accomplish much.

4. Are you praying Spirit-initiated prayers?

> "So Jesus said, 'When you lift up the Son of Man, then you will know that I am He, and I do nothing on My own initiative, but I speak these things as the Father taught Me. And He who sent Me is with Me; He has not left Me alone, for I always do the things that are pleasing to Him ... I speak the things which I have seen with My Father.'"[106]

As mentioned before, effective prayer is a loop that begins in heaven, travels through our hearts and minds, and returns to heaven. Jesus always did and said what His Father was initiating. The activity did not begin with the man, Jesus, but with the Father to the man and through the man. In this way, Jesus was constantly doing His Father's will and His prayers were perfectly aligned and stunningly effective.

---

[106]John 8:28-29, 38

If you want to be heard, listen first! Find out what the Spirit is saying and then pray in alignment with Him. God always answers prayers that He initiates!

5. Are you aligning your motives with God's?

> *"You ask and do not receive, because you ask with wrong motives, so that you may spend it on your pleasures. You adulteresses, do you not know that friendship with the world is hostility toward God? Therefore whoever wishes to be a friend of the world makes himself an enemy of God."*[107]

God gives no promise to bless our plans and our will, only His. In fact, He specifically reminds us that He will not hear and answer prayers that are selfish. Prayer is not aligning God with what we want, but spending time in His presence to align us to His will and plan.

6. Are you praying to be seen by men?

> *"When you pray, you are not to be like the hypocrites; for they love to stand and pray in the synagogues and on the street corners so that they may be seen by men. Truly I say to you, they have their reward in full."*[108]

Prayer that is prayed to be heard by men is only heard by men. It is easy to be so conscious of those around us that it drowns out our consciousness of the One to whom we are praying. Self-exalting

---

[107]James 4:3-4
[108]Matthew 6:5

prayers are not prayers at all. They are merely the babbling of a proud heart.

7. Are you harboring known sin?

"If I regard wickedness in my heart the Lord will not hear."[109]

No one prays who is not sinful and struggling with the ongoing battle against the world, the flesh, and the devil. But there is a difference between fighting against sin and harboring sin.

No one is perfect and no one prays perfectly. God knows our frame. He was tempted in all points like us, and we can "draw near with confidence to the throne of grace, so that we may receive mercy and find grace to help in time of need."[110] But often God will withhold His presence and His provision to get our attention so that we will deal with the sins that are destroying us and those around us.

8. Are you right with those around you?

"Therefore if you are presenting your offering at the altar, and there remember that your brother has something against you, leave your offering there before the altar and go; first be reconciled to your brother, and then come and present your offering."[111]

---

[109] Psalm 66:18
[110] Hebrews 4:16
[111] Matthew 5:23-24

The Father is aggressively concerned about the unity of His family. When His children are not right with each other, He takes any and every means to bring them back into right relationships.

Of all the things Jesus could have prayed for in His final, high priestly prayer, His great request was that we would be one with Him and one with each other.[112] He knows that we cannot hear Him and find His will if we are holding things in our hearts against others. Unforgiveness and enmity abort prayer and must be addressed as we approach the Throne.

9. Are you treating your mate with respect and honor?

> *"You husbands in the same way, live with your wives in an understanding way, as with someone weaker, since she is a woman; and show her honor as a fellow heir of the grace of life, so that your prayers will not be hindered."*[113]

Our homes are our first church. They are the proving grounds ... the laboratory for the things of God. We must first learn how to walk rightly with our family. God warns us that a dishonoring relationship with our spouse can destroy our effectiveness in prayer. This verse means exactly what it says. If someone dishonored your children callously, you would have a hard time listening to any request they would make of you. The same is true of God.

10. Are you praying with a proud, unbroken heart?

> *Two men went up into the temple to pray, one a Pharisee and the other a tax collector. The Pharisee stood and was*

---

[112]John 17:21
[113]1 Peter 3:7

*praying this to himself, "God, I thank You that I am not
like other people; swindlers, unjust, adulterers, or even
like this tax collector. I fast twice a week; I pay tithes of
all that I get."*

*But the tax collector, standing some distance away, was
even unwilling to lift up his eyes to heaven, but was beating
his breast, saying, "God, be merciful to me, the sinner!"*

*"I tell you, this man went to his house justified rather than
the other, for everyone who exalts himself will be humbled,
but he who humbles himself will be exalted."*[114]

God hates pride because it exalts us over Him. He has promised
He will "resist the proud."[115] This is a resistance you cannot afford.
A proud, judgmental, unbroken heart will hinder prayer. Our first
prayer should be, "Lord, be merciful to me, a sinner!"

11. Are you listening and gladly responding to God's Word?

*"He who turns away his ear from listening to the law, even
his prayer is an abomination.*[116]

The Bible is not a collection of man's thoughts about God. It is God
speaking! Since prayer needs to be God-initiated to be effective,
how can we pray if we are unwilling to listen and respond to what
He says?

It is an arrogant thing to believe that we could ignore what
God is saying and then expect Him to pay attention to what we are

[114]Luke 8:10-14
[115]James 4:6
[116]Proverbs 28:9

saying. God knows and longs for us to be effective in intercession for His kingdom's sake and knows this is best accomplished when we have a heart to obey Him. This is not speaking of perfection, of course, but a sincere heart that seeks to follow God.

12. Are you giving up in prayer?

> *"Now He was telling them a parable to show that at all times they ought to pray and not to lose heart."*[117]

The insightful parable Jesus shared in Luke 18 is a call to enduring prayer. George Mueller, the great pastor, orphanage director, and spiritual leader, said that he prayed all his life for two boyhood friends' salvation. When asked if he had stopped praying for them, he replied that he could not give up for God had assured him of the answer. One was saved at Mueller's funeral; the other six months after his death.

The timing of God's answers must be left in the hands of a Sovereign God who does all things perfectly. He knows what He's doing.

But as we think of these 12 hindrances, there is something we must never forget ...

GOD'S WILLINGNESS TO HEAR

The loss of hearing is debilitating. Our ears are one of the primary gates that give us the ability to know and respond to everything. The eyes, the nose, the mouth all aid us, as well as the sense of touch. But hearing is foundational.

---

[117] Luke 18:1

There are different levels of hearing. We hear thousands of sounds every day with no response. Our minds are conditioned to tune much of them out. We've labeled it "background noise." Our kids and some dads exercise what we could call "selective hearing." "Please take out the trash" is hardly ever heard the first time. "Let's go get ice cream" is heard with the slightest whisper.

God Hears

Our relationship with God is totally dependent on hearing. We must hear Him. Most don't. We have allowed the world's noise to so permeate us that our ears are rarely attuned to the "still small voice." Spiritual indifference and rebellion clog our ears. God is speaking all the time (even the heavens and earth speak continually), but we do not hear. This is our greatest tragedy.

But our relationship is also dependent on God being willing to hear us when we come to Him. This is the greater condescension, the greater mercy, and the greater promise. There is no possibility of a relationship if it is one-sided. We must hear God, but we must also be assured that He hears us.

Solomon's Prayer

When Solomon finished the building of the first temple in Jerusalem, his dedicatory prayer, found in 1 Kings 8, was a plea for God to hear. His whole prayer was "We need You and will need You, so God, please HEAR US when we pray!" Then Solomon recounts the various times when their prayers and God's hearing are so greatly needed.

- As I pray right now (vs. 28).

- When the people pray (vs. 30).

- When a man sins against his neighbor and comes backs to You and prays (vs. 30).

- When Your people are defeated before an enemy because they sinned against You and they turn and confess and pray (vs. 33).

- When the heavens are shut up and there is no rain because of our sins and we pray, confessing and returning to You (vs. 35).

- When there is famine or pestilence or plague or sickness and we pray (vs. 37-39).

- When the foreigner comes and prays (vs. 41-43).

- When we go to battle against an enemy and we pray (vs. 44).

- When Your people sin against You (for there is no man who does not sin) and you are angry and deliver us to an enemy and then we repent and pray (vs. 46-53).

Scroll through the prayer and you will notice that almost every human moment is covered. Solomon is essentially asking, "Lord, if we pray at any point of our need, will you hear?"

Notice that each prayer for God to hear is conditioned on several things. The people must repent, confess, return to God, and pray. God will not grant a proud prayer or a selfish prayer or prayer designed to advance a man's kingdom and not God's. His ear is deaf to those who will not listen to what He has said about their sin. And, of course, He will not hear what is not said. "You have not because you ask not," James 4:2 says. There is much in the Scripture about the conditions for effective prayer.

But, if we will come in humility and repentance and approach God in prayer, He has promised to hear us! It is the most amazing of all miracles. And, the One-Who-Hears has all the resources of heaven and earth at His disposal to meet our every need. God is a prayer-hearing and prayer-answering God!

CHAPTER 8

WHAT HELPS PRAYER?

MY DAD WAS A WONDERFUL PASTOR and leader for years, just like his dad. But dad was also a very good amateur carpenter (also just like his dad). His workshop in the garage was magical to me. Anything could be made with the right tools and a little time. I can close my eyes and smell the shavings coming off a sharp plane. He and I spent hours there.

Not only did I enjoy the work, but I also enjoyed being with him. We would talk about many things and along the way, he'd give me hints about woodwork and hints about life. Those helpful tips have carried me for decades.

Communion with God must be learned in the workshop of prayer. It should be natural to us, but sin has destroyed that possibility. Years of never talking to God must be replaced with new conversations with Him. And those conversations are always awkward at first, further complicated by the fact that God cannot be physically seen. Each of our five senses tell us this is not a reality. But the eyes of faith and the sure answers to prayer He gives can overcome this doubting reluctance over time.

So, come into the workshop and let's get some helpful hints on prayer, given in no particular order. Here are 12 short thoughts learned along the way that might change the dynamics of your lifelong communion with God.

1. LEARNING BY PRAYING

We can read about prayer, hear about prayer, think about prayer, but the greatest way to learn to pray is to pray! This means diving into the conversation. You must realize that there will be awkward moments—not on God's part, but yours—where you don't quite know what to do. But keep praying. Just like any conversation, in time your conversations will become natural and familiar with Him. Don't give up!

2. PRAYING THE BIBLE

One of the most helpful books on prayer is *Praying the Bible* by Donald Whitney. His insight into the need for Scripture-fed prayer is uncanny and his solutions are simple.

> Since prayer is talking with God, why don't people pray more? ... I maintain that people—truly born-again, genuinely Christian people—often do not pray simply because they do not feel like it. And the reason they don't feel like praying is that when they do pray, they tend to say the same old things about the same old things.
>
> When you've said the same old things about the same old things about a thousand times, how do you feel about saying them again? Did you dare to just think the "B" word? Yes, bored. We can be talking to the

most fascinating Person in the universe about the most important things in our lives and be bored to death.

As a result, a great many Christians conclude, "It must be me. Somethings wrong with me. If I get bored in something as important as prayer, then I must be a second-rate Christian."[118]

Whitney goes on to explain that the problem is not as much your desire in prayer as it is your method. And the method he proposes—experienced by himself and millions of others through the years—is the art of praying the Bible.

There are multiple prayers in the Scripture that can be prayed, of course. David's prayers in the Old Testament and Christ's and Paul's in the New Testament and many others give us incredible help. But the truth is that every Scripture can be turned into prayer. As you read your Bible daily, pause, and ask God to make the truths you encounter real in your experience. When you read of David's temptation, stop and pray that his failure would make you wise. When you are impressed by a Proverb, make it a prayer for yourself and others. Every principle, every command, every story can be—and is designed to be—a prayer point for you.

The man or woman who learns how to pray the Bible will have an inexhaustible supply in prayer.

---

[118] Donald Whitney, *Praying the Bible*

3. WORSHIPING IN PRAYER

Worship and prayer go hand-in-hand. Ask King David, one of the greatest pray-ers and greatest worshipers.

God loves to hear you sing. He loves to watch you write and journal. He loves to see you lift your hands because you cannot be still. Even a weak voice humbly lifted to Him translates to the sweetest music in heaven.

Use worship music or grab a hymnbook. Some of the greatest helps in prayer are found in old hymnbooks. Many great intercessors used them as a companion in their prayer closet.

Listen to some music and let the truths of the songs stimulate your praise. You can sing along and lift that song as a prayer to the only One worthy of our adoration.

4. LONG CONVERSATIONS AND RUNNING DIALOGUES

How do you talk to your best friend? Your conversation varies. Sometimes long conversations are needed … you need to "talk it out" with someone who will stay with you until the resolution comes.

But sometimes you just want to talk with them all day long. You call or text them often, enjoying all kinds of communication together.

We're made in God's image, so our conversation with others may provide a clue of what He desires with us in prayer. Sometimes we need long conversations and room should be made for this daily. But also, spiritual life is fueled by the running conversation with God. One man called these "bullet prayers." "Lord, give me wisdom as I head into this meeting." "Father, what should I do right now?" "Lord, thank You for the incredible glory of the sunset you've provided just for me!"

You'll discover as you grow in prayer that people who come into your mind at times are there for a reason. It is not a random thought for the serious Christian. God is bringing them to your mind to pray for them. If you pray, and talk to them later, you will often discover that your thought of them was not random, and your prayers were prompted by the Spirit Himself.

5. PRAYING INSTANTLY

Don Dudgeon was one of the original Elders at our church and a great man of God. But the first time I mentioned a need, he completely startled me. Without closing his eyes, he plunged headlong into a brief prayer for my situation. I was startled at first, but years with Don taught me to do the same.

When someone asks you to pray for them (or even if you don't but you sense a need) instantly pray. Why wait to bring God into the equation? Often if you delay you will lose the sense of urgency in prayer or forget to pray altogether.

> Above all—and again this I regard as most important
> of all—always respond to every impulse to pray. It
> is the work of the Holy Spirit. So never resist, never
> postpone it, never push it aside because you are busy.
> Give yourself to it, yield to it; and you will find not only
> that you have not been wasting time with respect
> to the matter with which you are dealing, but that
> actually it has helped you greatly in that respect.[119]

[119] Martyn Lloyd-Jones, *The Sermon on the Mount*

6. STUDYING PRAYING MEN AND WOMEN

Few things stir us to pray like being around men and women who know how to enter in. Their praying fuels ours and creates a hunger for a greater life of prayer. Find the men and women in your community who pray and ask them if you could periodically pray with them. They may not be the most famous among men, but they are the great heroes in heaven.

Tremendously helpful, and often more accessible, are the biographies of great men and women of prayer. Read the life of George Mueller, Hudson Taylor, Amy Carmichael, Praying John Hyde of India, Rees Howells, D.L. Moody, R.A. Torrey, Samuel Morris, David Brainerd, J.O. Fraser, William Duma, C.L. Culpepper, and Bertha Smith, to name a few. Devour every book that you can. Write in the back of each book the principles of prayer you see in their lives and then practice them in prayer.

7. PRAYING IN JESUS' NAME

One of the life-giving instructions from Christ as we pray is that we should pray "in His Name." This does not mean merely tagging a byline on the end of a prayer, but something far greater. It is that which assures us of answered prayers.

In the final hours before the cross, Jesus gives His final message to His disciples. They are fearful in this unnerving moment. They've left everything to follow Him and now He is saying that He's leaving. In John 14-16, Jesus gives what, in sports terms, could be considered a "locker room talk" (with far greater eternal results from the ultimate Coach!).

Jesus tells them not to be afraid. He's going away, but His

absence is only momentary. In His place He promised the coming of His Spirit who would be with them and in them, giving them all they would need. He tells them that they are going to do greater things than He did. These will not be greater in significance, but far greater in scope.

Along with the indwelling power of the Spirit and their continual abiding in Him, He gives them the practical step that will release the power of God. Four times in these three chapters, He reminds them that the path to greater works is through prayer.

There are several instructions to make this prayer effective. We must abide in Christ. We must let His Word abide in us so that He can direct our prayers and bring our thinking in alignment with His. But we must also pray "in His Name." He mentions this five times in these passages, emphasizing it's importance.

> "Truly, truly, I say to you, he who believes in Me, the works that I do, he will do also; and greater works than these he will do; because I go to the Father. Whatever you ask **in My name,** that will I do, so that the Father may be glorified in the Son. If you ask Me anything **in My name,** I will do it. If you love Me, you will keep My commandments." [120]

> "If you abide in Me, and My words abide in you, ask whatever you wish, and it will be done for you. My Father is glorified by this, that you bear much fruit, and so prove to be My disciples." [121]

---

[120]John 14:12-15 *(emphasis mine)*
[121]John 15:7-8 *(emphasis mine)*

*"You did not choose Me but I chose you, and appointed
you that you would go and bear fruit, and that your fruit
would remain, so that whatever you ask of the Father **in
My name** He may give to you."* [122]

*"In that day you will not question Me about anything. Truly,
truly, I say to you, if you ask the Father for anything **in
My name**, He will give it to you. Until now you have asked
for nothing **in My name**; ask and you will receive, so that
your joy may be made full."* [123]

So what does this all-important disclaimer mean? When a nation
sends an ambassador to a foreign country they go in the name of
the President of that nation and its people. Alone, they are just
an ordinary person with no powers of their own. But when they
come "in the name of" their country they carry all the authority
of those they represent.

Of course, to be effective , this Ambassador must be trustwor-
thy. He must know what the wishes of his Commander-in-Chief
are. And, he must behave in such a way that does not discredit
those he represents. But when he speaks, he speaks in the name
of his President. When he asks, he asks on behalf of his President.
He carries the authority of their name.

There is no name higher than Jesus' name! It is the Name
before which, one day, every knee will bow. As believers, we come
to the Throne Room not on the basis of our name, but Christ's.
His sacrificial death and resurrection have paved the way for us to
come. We have a right to be there, not because of our perfection,

---

[122]John 15:16 *(emphasis mine)*
[123]John 16:23-24 *(emphasis mine)*

but our union with Him and His invitation to come before the King. We enter in His name. The more we read His Word the more we know what He wants. Our will and prayers align with His. And, we pray with the right motivation—not to glorify ourselves, but to make His name known.

The wonderful pastor and teacher, Ron Dunn, said that he once had a terrible day. He came to the end of the day and simply could not pray. He sensed God saying to him, "Ron, if you had a great time with Me this morning, had walked with me all day, and had ministered to dozens of people, would you feel ready to pray?" Ron replied, "Yes, Lord, I believe I would." To which the Lord replied, "Ron, you're praying in YOUR name—on the basis of your goodness. The only way you can approach me is on the basis of my Son's name and merits."

Think of this honor and this granted authority! We come as a representative of the King of kings. We come because Christ said we could enter the Throne Room. We ask on His behalf for His glory and the advancement of His kingdom. And we live to honor Him well and see His agenda accomplished.

When you have prayed through a request so fully that you can genuinely say, "Lord, I come in the name of Christ who said I could come and I ask this not for MY name, but Yours," then prepare to see greater works.

8. PRAYER LISTS

Some think that having prayer lists makes praying mechanical. But our mind is quick to wander in prayer. Developing lists of topics such as family members, pastors, missionaries, lost people,

Christian friends, government leaders, etc. allows us to take a topic a day to direct our prayers. We may feel led to pray for some of these lists every day. Many have found it helpful to categorize these lists and pray for certain categories on certain days.

If you've never tried it and are having trouble focusing in prayer, you might be amazed at this helpful suggestion. A notebook or simple cards can be used. Now, there are prayer apps that can be used as well and are incredibly helpful.

Don't make fun of those who use lists. Somewhat tedious prayer is always better than mind-wandering prayer.

9. PRAYING WITH OTHERS

Most of the praying we see in the New Testament was done in groups. Like sticks of wood that increase a fire, mutual intercession aids us in praying. Someone comes into the group and is distracted, but another is focused and ready to pray. One is discouraged, but another intercessor's prayers lift them before the meeting is over. We fuel each other in prayer.

If you are not praying with others, you must. Start a group; join a group. Ask a godly older man or woman who you know is an intercessor to train you by praying with you.

As a pastor for over 50 years, I have been astounded to discover countless pastors who never pray with their leaders and staff. Their group prayer is often a tag at the beginning or end of a meeting. How can we possibly expect to let the Head of the church lead His body if we are not talking to Him? How can we build genuine unity in our church teams without united prayer? What are we training others to be if we never train them in prayer?

Also, real unity—the kind that moves mountains—cannot be gained by administration or tasks alone. Get a group of people into the presence of God in sustained, well-led prayer and unity will be automatic. There will be a depth of unity that cannot be experienced any other way.

10. LEADING PRAYER

At some point, you may be asked to lead a prayer meeting. One of the greatest tragedies of the church is boring prayer meetings! It happens all the time. There are multiple reasons why this may be happening. The leader may not understand that prayer meetings must be led. The Holy Spirit should be the leader, but an earthly leader who is prepared, thoughtful, and has an ear to heaven is the vessel through which He works. If you are called to lead a prayer meeting ... LEAD! If you don't know how to lead a prayer meeting ... LEARN! Find someone who leads prayer meetings well and humbly seek their help.

Many pastors have never seen an effective prayer meeting modeled. If they knew better, they'd do better. Take the model of Jesus in Matthew 6 that we've outlined. Walk people into God's presence and then use each prayer movement. Don't let prayer drag on with long periods of dead space. Stop before they're quite through. Leave them hungry for more prayer.

11. POSTURE IN PRAYER

Posture is important (or so my mother said!). It indicates things. It also puts you in the right position to do what needs to be done.

A pole-vaulter would not start by lying on his back. He could not reach his destination well from there.

Multiple postures in prayer are mentioned in Scripture such as standing, hands raised, head bowed, head lifted up, sitting, kneeling, walking, and lying prostrate on the floor. Each of these signifies something and each should be considered appropriate when needed.

Sometimes when I am praying, I have found no break-through until I get on my face before God. I don't know why, but that has been real in my experience for 50 years. Perhaps it's because it's the lowest point of humility before God.

There are times when praying is hard, and the mind is wandering. Walking around and praying aloud is needed.

Here is the important lesson: position yourself where the Spirit prompts, even in public. Nothing would thrill an authentic pastor's heart more than seeing one of his people spontaneously kneeling during their gathering. You will rarely go wrong if you take a humble posture before God.

12. RECORDING PRAYERS

George Mueller left a legacy that will probably challenge believers until the Lord returns. He was a man of great faith and unceasing prayer. Never mentioning a need to any man, he pastored a church and developed an orphanage that fed, housed, and trained up to 2,000 children annually.

Mueller felt the secret was Word-fed, believing prayer. "I live in the spirit of prayer," Mueller wrote. "I pray as I walk, when I lie down and when I rise, and the answers are always coming."

He was so desirous of showing the world that God was a "prayer-hearing and prayer-answering God" that he meticulously recorded over 50,000 answers to prayer that he received, 30,000 of which were answered on the same day or hour in which they were prayed. These answers were recorded and shared at the end of every year in his published "Records of the Lord's Dealings." Most of what we know of Mueller's life of prayer comes from those records.

If we journal and keep accounts to glorify ourselves we're in trouble. But recording our prayers and God's answers for the purpose of magnifying God is extremely valuable. Think of the legacy such records would leave! It could inspire and train the next generations, just as the Psalmist encouraged.

> *"We will not conceal them from their children, but tell to the generation to come the praises of the* LORD, *and His strength and His wondrous works that He has done."*[124]

All of us have much to learn in prayer. But we can be grateful that we have the ultimate Teacher and the examples of countless men and women who've gone before us and prayed successfully. We are blessed with the Word of God to guide us and the Spirit to empower us. We have all we need to grow into men and women of unceasing prayer. It should be our greatest joy and highest privilege.

---

[124] Psalm 78:4

AS YOU BEGIN TO PRAY …

IT WAS THE RAREST OF PRIVILEGES. They were unaware of its glory for they were the first to walk this way. They would have been shocked to discover that, of all those who followed, they were the only entrants to this place—the only ones who would enjoy such company.

The splendor of their garden home was so vibrant it could be tasted. The richest of fruits graced every tree. Hundreds of birds clothed in downy grace swept through the air in perfect rhythm. They filled the air with their unfettered hymns.

Lions and lambs roamed the woods with no animosity. Soft, fertile ground was easy on their feet providing warm texture.

Brilliant sunlight streamed through the canopy above and the night brought coolness and rest and the matchless display of the heavens.

"Every day, my children, I will meet you here," the Creator said. "We will walk and talk together. There is nothing I will not tell you; nothing I will not provide for you. And when you don't see me, I am always present. If you speak, I will answer without a moment's pause."

"All that you see, except one tree and its fruit, has been created for you. Everything in this Garden will nourish you and be unceasingly replenished. There is an inexhaustible supply."

And so, the man and wife would wake each day, eat the rich food that was everywhere present, and go about their work. Theirs were fulfilling tasks—free from excessive strain—for it was easy in a garden where there was not a hint of darkness, no touch of evil.

Their love for each other was perfect, untainted with the anger and suspicion, disrespect and mistrust that would later come.

But the richest moments of the day—the hours that filled their hearts until they felt they would burst in their chests—happened in the cool of the day when they would walk together with the Majestic One. How do you describe a conversation with One who is altogether lovely? Perfect in wisdom, matchless in grace? One who is greater than all yet interested in the smallest details of your life?

These daily conversations breathed life into their souls. After each, they always knew what they were to do next, for He was the perfect Leader. But it was not mere instruction. There was laughter and joy, encouragement and hope. Some days He would show them the glories of the Garden. He would describe the intricate designs of birds and animals. The pattern of each leaf. Even the air about them was perfectly designed.

Other days they would simply walk in silence, enjoying the company of the One they loved. Their hearts were settled, their souls at peace. Everything they needed, every moment of each day was provided through their union with Him.

They did not know that there was a Tempter, waiting silently in the shadows. And on the most tragic of days he came. His intent was not merely to destroy them, wrenching them from their Father, but to destroy the Father Himself. With a simple, twisted temptation, he led them to doubt God's truthfulness ... and they fell.

After the Enemy's deception and their unbelief, the conversations radically changed. An awkwardness invaded their relationship. They felt their nakedness. They tasted the bitterness of their disobedience. The new-found experience of guilt was heavy. The rest was gone. The Creator knew that if they tasted of the tree that would give them immortality, they would live in this fallen existence forever. So, He banished them from the Garden and closed the door.

They were taken from this matchless place and their remaining days would be spent in the wearisome toil of their sin. But their greatest loss was their lack of communion with Him.

But God's plan was not thwarted by Satan's work and man's sin. A promised One would come. His serpent-crushing, saving work was prophesied at the moment of their sin. And when He came, He would make a way for all to come into the Father's presence and know Him once again. To walk with Him; to hear His voice; to regain what once was lost. One day the door would open, and the Garden would be fully restored ... and the conversation would continue with no interruption. Unceasing prayer, unceasing love, unceasing joy.

This glorious walk with God is now open for us with all its riches. We can walk in the Garden of His presence. We can experience now in part what we will one day experience fully in a new heaven and new earth. But for all who long for Him, He invites us now to come.

And the doorway through which we enter is *simply prayer.*

GROUP DISCUSSION QUESTIONS

Walk through the discussion questions listed, but make sure you leave time for group prayer at the end. Take the things you're learning and "Pray them in!" asking God to make the truths that your learning real in your experience and the experience of your group.

Chapter 1: WHY PRAY?

1. What caught your attention in this chapter?

2. Do you agree that "The most powerful person in the room is the one who prays?" Why or why not?

3. In the list of reasons why many do not value prayer, what resonates with you the most?

4. Is it hard for you to believe that God really wants your prayers? Why or why not?

5. How could prayer help you interpret life? Understand the things that are happening around you?

6. Share about an experience where you felt your prayers were helping someone else.

7. Share about a time when talking with the Father calmed your heart and brought peace.

Chapter 2: HOW DO WE ENTER IN?

1. Do you have a conscious sense of God's presence when you begin praying? If so, what has helped you gain this?

2. Read together Matthew 6:5-9. Which of these five elements in "entering in" spoke to you the most and why?

3. What did you learn about sincerity in prayer?

4. What did you learn about seclusion in prayer?

5. What did you learn about simplicity in prayer?

6. What did you learn about simple faith in prayer?

7. What did you learn about entering as a son or daughter?

Chapter 3: WHAT DO WE PRAY?

1. Have you ever had a hard time knowing what to pray? What has helped you overcome this?

2. Why should we begin our prayers with adoration?

3. Why is it important in prayer to align our will and prayers with God's will? What happens if we don't take time for this alignment?

4. What are some things today—some needs—that you need to give God access to?

5. Why is immediate confession important in our prayer life? Why is it important to clear our conscience with others?

6. Where is the ground of your life that Satan attacks most often? Where are you the most vulnerable?

7. Share about a time when you had to come to a fresh place of surrender to the Lordship of Christ and what resulted because of this surrender.

Chapter 4: WHEN SHOULD WE PRAY?

1. Do you think often about the fact that you are facing a real Enemy? What do you think a lack of awareness of Satan's activity could do?

2. Read through the description of our Enemy found in Ephesians 6:10-13. What does this tell you about the enemies we're fighting?

3. What are some of the schemes Satan uses against you?

4. Share about a time when you needed the Lord to be your strength. How did you practically take the step to "be strong in the Lord and the strength of His might?" (Ephesians 6:10).

5. Walk through and discuss the four "all's" found in Ephesians 6:18. What do each of these mean to you in prayer?

6. Why do you think we are often unaware of our mission?

7. What would happen if we were praying for each other daily for boldness in our witness for Christ? How could this affect our lives and the lives of others?

Chapter 5: WHAT IS EXTRAORDINARY PRAYER?

1. What do you think are the signs that we are in a National Spiritual Emergency?

2. Do you think we need to see revival in the church and spiritual awakening among the lost? What are the differences between these two things?

3. Read slowly through the title of Jonathan Edwards book. Which phrase in that title impacts you the most and why?

4. What do you think would be the evidence that you and your group were experiencing "extraordinary prayer?"

5. Do you think FOUNDATIONAL Prayer is evident in most churches? Where have you seen this true and why?

6. Do you see signs of desperate prayer growing in our nation?

7. What do you think it would take to create a movement of extraordinary prayer across our nation?

Chapter 6: HOW SHOULD WE PRAY FOR REVIVAL AND AWAKENING?

1. What voices do you hear currently that are sounding the call for revival and awakening?

2. What are the signs that desperation is increasing and a cry for God's reviving work is occurring?

3. Why is repentance so important to the work of God in revival?

4. Is there increased spiritual activity occurring around us? What do you see?

5. Do you find yourself proclaiming the message of the gospel more? If not, what is it that creates our fear of proclaiming Christ?

6. What role does persevering prayer play in revival? Why should we continue praying, even when we don't see the desired results immediately?

7. Take a moment and pray the prayer at the close of the chapter together aloud. This would be a good prayer to memorize and use in your daily time with God!

Chapter 7: WHAT HINDERS PRAYER?

1. Have you ever considered that there could be hindrances to your prayers?

2. Of the twelve hindrances listed, which speaks to you the most?

3. How do you think harboring sin affects your prayers and why?

4. How do you think harboring sin against your mate affects your prayers and why?

5. Do you really believe that God wants to hear our prayers? What does He have to gain by listening to His children?

6. Read through the list of Solomon's prayers. Which of these prayers seems especially appropriate right now?

7. Pause and pray together. Thank God that He hears our prayers and cry out for what is on your heart.

Chapter 8: WHAT HELPS PRAYER?

1. How does the Bible help you in your praying?

2. What has been your experience in talking with God throughout the day? A running conversation?

3. What books have you read that have helped you in your prayer life and why?

4. What do you think it means to pray "in Jesus' name?"

5. Do you use lists in your prayer times? Does it help and why?

6. What is the benefit of regularly praying with others?

7. What is the single greatest thing you have learned through reading *Simply Prayer?*

OTHER BOOKS BY BILL ELLIFF

BOOKS

The Presence Centered Church

Whitewater
Navigating the Rapids of Church Conflict

A Small Book About the Large Ways of a Powerful God
Taught to a Weak Creature in His Brief Life
Preparing Him for an Endless Eternity
12 Life Lessons We All Must Learn

OneCry!
A Nationwide Call for Spiritual Awakening
(Byron Paulus and Bill Elliff)

GRACEFUL TRUTH SERIES BOOKS

The Line of Faith
40 Days to Deepened Dependency

The Essential Presence
40 Days to Increased Intimacy with God

Prayer with No Intermission
40 Days to Unceasing Prayer

BOOKLETS

Forgiveness
Healing the Harbored Hurts of Your Heart

Lifting Life's Greatest Load
How to Gain and Maintain a Clear Conscience

Turning the Tide
Having More Children Who Follow Christ
(Holly Elliff with Bill Elliff)

The Power and Joy of Biblical Fasting

50 Marks of a Man of God

Personal Revival Checklist

Everyman

All Resources Available at www.BillElliff.org